IMAGES
of America

PORT ARANSAS

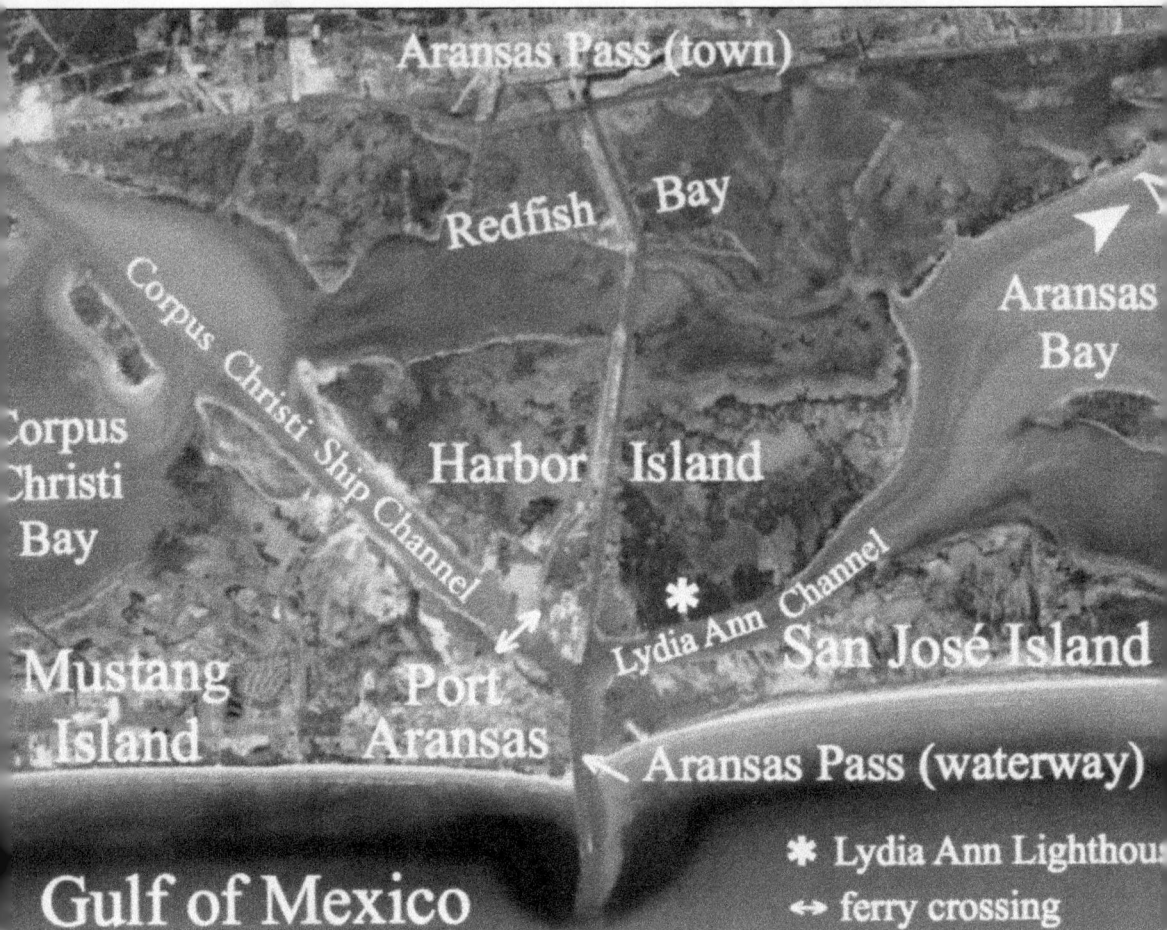

Aransas Pass (town)

Redfish Bay

Aransas Bay

Corpus Christi Ship Channel

Corpus Christi Bay

Harbor Island

Lydia Ann Channel

San José Island

Mustang Island

Port Aransas

Aransas Pass (waterway)

Gulf of Mexico

✳ Lydia Ann Lighthouse
↔ ferry crossing

The map above shows Port Aransas and its close-by environs. Reference to this map will be helpful when reading the text.

ON THE COVER: This photograph from around 1960 was taken in the foredunes of the Gulf of Mexico beach that is contiguous to Port Aransas. These Port Aransas residents are, from left to right, Phyllis Sims, Linda Mathews, Betty Revell, Dorothy Roberts, and Ann Studeman (seated). The image was a publicity shot used to promote a town function, most likely a fishing tournament. (Courtesy of the Port Aransas Preservation and Historical Association.)

IMAGES
of America

PORT ARANSAS

J. Guthrie Ford and Mark Creighton

ARCADIA
PUBLISHING

Copyright © 2010 by J. Guthrie Ford and Mark Creighton
ISBN 978-1-5316-5253-1

Published by Arcadia Publishing
Charleston, South Carolina

Library of Congress Control Number: 2010938466

For all general information, please contact Arcadia Publishing:
Telephone 843-853-2070
Fax 843-853-0044
E-mail sales@arcadiapublishing.com
For customer service and orders:
Toll-Free 1-888-313-2665

Visit us on the Internet at www.arcadiapublishing.com

CONTENTS

ACKNOWLEDGMENTS

We thank Georganna Creighton and Pamalee Ford for reviewing the images that were considered for this book and critically reading the associated captions. Their observations and comments were very helpful.

We also acknowledge the Port Aransas Preservation and Historical Association for permitting access to its archive of historical images. This work could not have been accomplished without that resource.

Unless otherwise noted, all images appear courtesy of the Port Aransas Preservation and Historical Association.

INTRODUCTION

Port Aransas is a community on the north tip of Mustang Island, Texas. It is the only community on the island. Port Aransas is colloquially known as "Port A," a moniker appearing regularly in this book. Mustang Island will be referred to as simply "Mustang" or the "Island."

The Port Aransas story cannot be told outside the context of Mustang Island. Eighteen miles long, it is one of seven named barrier islands along the Texas coast. Once a submerged, coast-hugging shoal, Mustang emerged from the Gulf of Mexico 3,500 years ago. About two millennia ago, the Island became a seasonal home to one of the native peoples of Texas. During the chilly months, the nomadic Karankawa gathered oysters and took fish by bow and arrow.

Mustang Island was settled when the Robert A. Mercer family arrived in 1855, after the Karankawa had left the area. The Mercers built their homestead on the head of the island, and a small settlement soon took root around the Mercer nucleus. Further growth, however, was interrupted by Civil War violence, forcing the islanders to leave until the end of the war.

During Reconstruction, the economy of Mustang Island expanded when people began raising cattle for export to Northern markets. When the cattle industry waned in the 1870s, the economy shifted to the export of redfish, turtle, and wild duck—all legal table fare then. The latter part of the 19th century saw the start of sport fishing in the close-by waters of the Aransas Pass (see map). The pass was home to large schools of tarpon, a sport fish valued because of its enthusiastic fighting behavior when hooked. Some Mustang Islanders began earning money by rowing fishermen out to the tarpon grounds, marking the birth of the current fishing guide and charter boat businesses. A guide takes parties to the bays to fish; a charter boat captain takes parties offshore—to the Gulf of Mexico—to fish.

In 1888, the Mustang Island community of approximately 100 people took the name Ropesville. That appellation reflected the islanders' enthusiasm for a fast-talking promoter Elihu Ropes, who promised them numerous economic advantages, none of which were realized. Disenchanted, the residents of Ropesville changed the name of their village in 1896 to Tarpon, reflecting the importance of that fish to their economic well-being; sport fishermen from near and far were coming to Mustang Island to catch the fighting tarpon.

The town name Tarpon, however, was not long lived. The development of a seaport on nearby Harbor Island portended stable and well-paying maritime jobs, and in the enthusiasm of the day, the townsfolk dropped Tarpon in 1910 in favor of Port Aransas. However, not then—or ever—has Port Aransas been a commercial shipping port. The name reflects the town's excitement in 1910 about the maritime economy promised by the neighboring seaport.

The 270 people of Port Aransas were looking at a bright future in 1912. The bustling Harbor Island seaport was a major point for exporting Texas cotton, and some Port Aransans worked the machines that pressed the cotton into bales, some loaded the bales onto ships taking the cotton to French and English clothing mills, and some manned the tugboats that moved the ships in and out of the port.

In addition to those maritime jobs, Port Aransas stayed committed to its world-class tarpon fishing. The Port Aransas Commercial Club created advertising campaigns to bring fishermen to Mustang Island. An enterprising club member even composed the words that became Port A's slogan, "Where They Bite Every Day." The running joke is that this refers to mosquitoes, not fish.

The Port Aransas maritime economy began to shrink in 1914 when the European cotton ships were assigned to other duties relevant to World War I. In the midst of that economic slide, the weather dealt two deadly blows. A 1916 hurricane damaged the Harbor Island seaport, and barely had repairs been made when an even more powerful hurricane laid utter waste to the port in 1919, resulting in layoffs and lost jobs. The coup de grâce to Port A's faltering maritime economy came in 1926 when the Corpus Christi ship channel opened. Compared to the Harbor Island seaport, the Corpus Christi port was larger and had better transportation systems for moving cargoes. Ships now steamed right past the deserted Harbor Island docks en route to Corpus. The maritime economy of Port Aransas collapsed, and in 1926 the town was in serious economic straits.

While the townsfolk still had revenue from the sport fishing guide business, smart people knew that that revenue alone was not sufficient to ensure a stable and growing economy. What was needed was the larger tourist paradigm wherein sportsmen would bring their families to Port Aransas. While dad fished, mom and the children would enjoy the beach, then everyone would browse a shop or two, eat at a restaurant, and of course rent a cottage to sleep in. In other words, Port A needed a tourist industry in the fullest sense of the word.

Family-based tourism could only be achieved if there was easy vehicular access to Mustang Island, which was finally achieved in the late 1920s by way of a unique causeway and an innovative railroad. Indeed, even despite the Great Depression, the 350 Port Aransans were, tourist-wise, doing pretty well. President Roosevelt coming to fish in 1937 gave the town phenomenal publicity. Four years after that, however, America entered World War II and tourism took a back seat as Port A became a strategic military base—Fort Port Aransas—on the Texas coast.

The story after the war is of Port Aransas changing from a small place with a smattering of mom-and-pop stores and motor courts to a thriving tourist town of more than 3,300 people. (The 2010 census is anticipated to be 20 percent higher). The story involves hosting nationally recognized fishing tournaments, being a spring break locale for the college crowd and families, a well-kept beach, noted bird-watching facilities, a fine museum, and an annual beach extravaganza featuring internationally recognized sand sculptors.

The traditional model of transient visitors coming to Port A from Texas and northern states has recently expanded to include people coming here to settle permanently. As the 21st century unfolds, growth, change, and social diversity are the watchwords for Port Aransas, Texas. The next few decades promise to be quite a ride and worlds apart from the sleepy little fishing village of yesteryear.

One

A SANDY HISTORY STAGE

The history of Mustang Island and Port Aransas has two levels. The changes in the Island and town over time—the focus of this book—and, secondly, the roles the Island and town have played in histories having national and international scope. This chapter addresses that broader perspective.

Mustang Island has a link to the human history of this continent. The Island was once home to the ancestors of the first North American inhabitants, humans that came from Asia 20,000 years ago. They came onto Mustang about two millennia ago. The Island was seen early in the European exploration of the New World. In 1519, the Mustang shoreline was sketched by Alonzo Álvarez de Pineda on the first map of the Texas coast.

Mustang Island and its Aransas Pass, the natural waterway off the north shore, either played into or witnessed historical events during the 19th century. The spark that ignited the Texas Revolution sailed through the pass in 1835, and a decade later an American army fortified Mustang Island on its way to fight the Mexican-American War. In 1849, some of the forty-niners heading to California came through the Aransas Pass to take the southern overland route to the gold fields.

The fury of the American Civil War visited Mustang Island, and the strife caused the islanders to leave until the end of the conflict. During postwar Reconstruction, the federal government took an interest in the Island because the Aransas Pass waterway was the gateway to a maritime economy for the coastal Southwest. That attention revealed the pass to be a dangerous marine environment, leading the government to commission a U.S. Life Saving Station—a forerunner of the Coast Guard—that began operations on the Island in 1880.

In the 20th century, Port Aransas hosted Pres. Franklin Roosevelt on his 1937 tarpon fishing trip, and a few years later the town became an armed bastion, Fort Port Aransas, during World War II.

For being such small places, Mustang Island and Port Aransas have been sandy stages for a fair bit of history.

The nomadic Karankawa people were the first humans on Mustang Island. Spending fall and winter on the Island, the Karankawa subsisted on aquatic plants, oysters, and fish, the latter taken by bow and arrow in shallow areas. When Mustang was settled in 1855, the Karankawa had migrated elsewhere. (Courtesy of Matagorda County Museum, Bay City, Texas.)

Horses came to Mustang Island from shipwrecks and neighboring Spanish settlements. These animals produced herds of mustangs, giving rise to the Island's name; some believe the Spanish name was *Isla Mesteño*. Settlement of the Island saw eradication of the wild horses because they competed with settlers' livestock for food.

The dashing figure at right is Jean Lafitte. Around 1819, this famous buccaneer built a fort on the tip of San José Island, which lies just north of Mustang Island. The Lafitte crew lit bogus distress fires on the Mustang beach to lure ships into the shallow surf where they became easy prey. A lasting Port Aransas myth is that Lafitte buried a treasure in the dunes that has never been found. (Courtesy of the Jewish Journal of Greater Los Angeles.)

When the Mexican province of Texas was on the verge of open revolt, it was up to Gen. Martín Perfecto de Cos to restore order. In September 1835, he sent 500 troops sailing through the Aransas Pass, and upon landing they marched inland to arrest rebel leaders. That event so inflamed Texians that two weeks later the fighting began. The spark that ignited the Texas Revolution had come through the Aransas Pass waterway.

A national goal in the 1840s was manifest destiny, the expansion of America to the Pacific Ocean. To achieve this, the United States sought to secure the Rio Grande River as an international boundary but Mexico aggressively opposed it. To counter that threat, President Polk, in 1845, sent an army under Gen. Zachary Taylor through the Aransas Pass to Corpus Christi, where the Taylor army encamped (see image above). To stop the Mexicans from coming through the pass to attack his encampment, Taylor put a fort on Mustang Island. The United States won the Mexican-American War in 1848 and a year later gold was discovered in California. Mustang Island then saw the next phase of manifest destiny as some forty-niners sailed through the Aransas Pass to begin their cross-country journey to the "Golden State." (Courtesy of Corpus Christi Public Library.)

Mustang Island was settled in 1855 by Robert and Agnes Mercer with offspring John, Edward, and Mary Agnes. Naming their homestead *El Mar Rancho* (sea ranch), the family subsisted on beef and dairy cattle, as well as ducks and oysters from area waters. The house pictured here around 1882 belonged to either John or Edward Mercer. It was constructed of driftwood and imported lumber; Mustang Island was treeless. The Mercers were ship pilots who guided vessels from the Gulf of Mexico through the perilous Aransas Pass. They used the roof lookout to spot ships requiring their service. The family grouping below shows the Mercers' wives and children appearing as the Texas coastal pioneers they were.

During the Civil War, Lt. John Kittredge of the Federal navy captained the USS *Arthur*—a bark sailing ship, as pictured here—to Mustang Island in order to blockade the Aransas Pass against southern shipping. In February 1862, Federal sailors confiscated Mustang livestock for their food supply, which caused some islanders to fire on them. Kittredge responded by torching houses, causing Mustang Island to be abandoned until the war ended.

Lt. John Kittredge's presence on the coast eventually led to a famous battle at close-by Corpus Christi in August 1862. This illustration shows Kittredge's naval force engaging Confederate artillery commanded by Maj. Alfred Hobby. Unable to silence those guns, the Federals withdrew, and a month later Kittredge was captured while ashore. (Courtesy of Corpus Christi Public Library.)

With Kittredge gone, the Confederates established Fort Semmes, an artillery emplacement on Mustang Island. In November 1863, approximately 1,500 Federal infantrymen attacked the fort, causing it to surrender by lowering the unusual Rebel flag shown here (red field, blue diagonals, yellow stars). The flag hung in a state office in Augusta, Maine, before being returned to Texas in 1928.

Postwar Reconstruction was economically robust along the Texas coast. There was extensive maritime traffic going through Aransas Pass, which carried whole cattle and cattle products (e.g., tallow and hides) to Northern markets. The pass was a dangerous waterway, and in November 1876, the fashionable passenger steamship *Mary* sank attempting to transit it. A daring rescue saved the ship's company. (Courtesy of Espey, Huston, and Associates.)

The publicized sinking of the *Mary* persuaded the government to take a close look at safety issues at the Aransas Pass. In 1878, the U.S. Life Saving Service, the forerunner of the U.S. Coast Guard, commissioned this station on Mustang Island where Port Aransas was eventually located. Behind the crew is the trailered lifeboat that was rolled to the water for launching.

Nicaragua, a Mexican tramp steamer, lost power in a heavy gale and wrecked off the Padre Island beach (just south of Mustang) in 1912. The crew was rescued by personnel of the U.S. Life Saving Station. The ship's engine was sabotaged by Mexican loyalists believing that the vessel was serving a revolutionary cause. A Padre Island cattle rancher furnished his house with tables and chairs salvaged from the *Nicaragua*. The ship's rusting hulk is shown in this early-1930s photograph.

Port Aransas was in the national eye early in World War II when a German submarine was spotted close to Mustang Island in January 1942. The event fully engaged the town in the great conflict and the U.S. Army, Navy, and Coast Guard all had a presence in Port A. The U.S. Coast Guard initiated the Ports, Waterways, and Coastal Security (PWCS) mission; pictured here are two elements of that mission. The beach patrol guarded the length of Mustang Island against the landing of German saboteurs. The two Coast Guard patrol vessels monitored activity around the docks of a nearby strategic oil depot, as well as checked to see that vessels transiting the Aransas Pass were authorized to do so—a permit was required to go into the gulf.

17

The 9/11 attacks on the United States resulted in the Coast Guard being assigned to the Department of Homeland Security. For the first time since World War II, the Port Aransas station returned to a wartime footing. Just as it had in 1942, station personnel began carrying out Ports, Waterways, and Coastal Security missions. Of course, during the War on Terrorism there was no threat of terrorists coming ashore by submarine, so there was no beach patrol. Instead the PWCS missions are to provide security for high-asset vessels transiting the Aransas Pass and to prevent vessels bringing terrorists or terrorist assets into the United States. The high-speed Coast Guard response boat shown here is a primary tool in conducting these homeland security missions.

Two

WIND AND
WAVE MONSTERS

A book about Port Aransas must address the two most frequently asked questions about its history: what was the worst hurricane and when was the last hurricane? This aspect of town history is presented early, so to devote the rest of this book to more constructive and uplifting historical topics.

Members of the Robert A. Mercer family, Mustang Island's first settlers in 1855, compiled thousands of diary entries that are collectively known as the Mercer Logs. Most entries begin and end with weather notations; for instance, from an entry in November, 1866: "This day begins with wind east moderate . . . So ends this day with a light southeast wind."

Living mere feet above sea level, it was, and still is of course, smart to keep a sharp weather eye. Not long after settling Mustang Island, the Mercers survived a storm ("storm" is vernacular for "hurricane" on the Texas coast) that saw the Gulf of Mexico rush madly through their home and drown their livestock.

In this chapter, photo-narrative information is presented about the following major storms: 1919, 1942, 1945, Hurricane Carla in 1961, and Hurricane Celia in 1970. (Hurricane naming did not begin until 1950.) The 1919 storm had a tremendous storm surge, which is the flooding water a storm pushes onshore, comparable to a tsunami. The August 1942 hurricane damaged the military installations on the Island so severely that the U.S. War Department disallowed any repairs until the end of hurricane season on November 30. Some parts of Port Aransas were still being repaired from the 1942 storm when another hurricane smashed ashore three years later.

Paradoxically, Hurricane Carla in 1961 and Hurricane Celia in 1970 each had a positive side. Carla wiped out the town honky-tonks and illegal gambling and vice joints—after World War II Port Aransas had become quite a party town. When the townsfolk rebuilt, they transformed Port Aransas into a family-centered community. Celia proved to developers that structures built to withstand extreme weather have a chance of surviving a major hurricane, and that revelation led to a period of significant development and growth.

Board up the windows and head for high ground! Howling winds and big water start now.

This is Port Aransas after the 1961 Hurricane Carla. The waves rolling in have changed the town from a place fronting on water to a place covered by water. Normally the water is only between the two rows of buildings. The extensive flooding was caused by the massive volume of seawater that the hurricane pushed ashore; in hurricane parlance, this inundation is referred to as the storm surge. Although this photograph was taken one day after the storm, the high water remained, creating a very bad long-term consequence. The standing water had a good, long time to soak into the floors and walls of structures so that even after the water resided and things dried out, corrosion had occurred and black mold was growing in unseen places. Many structures consumed by these aftereffects must eventually be razed, increasing the time it takes for a community to recover from a hurricane; in some cases, it can take years.

The September 1919 hurricane had a monstrous storm surge, washing thousands of yards of sand back from the beach. Once it was dug out, this dormered house with the flagpole served as the U.S. Coast Guard station in lieu of the official station that was destroyed by the storm. The structure, called the Mercer house, remarkably went on to survive every hurricane that came its way and today serves as the Port Aransas Museum.

Neighboring Corpus Christi was the scene of this extraordinary field of lumber—as high as a two-story building—salvaged after the 1919 hurricane. The storm surge that swept over this city's low-lying North Beach killed an estimated 1,000 people. In Port Aransas, Rockport, and Aransas Pass, the storm claimed five, eight, and two deaths, respectively. (Courtesy of Murphy Givens and Jim Moloney.)

John E. Cotter, one of the Island's first fishing and hunting guides, lived in this classic coast house. The wraparound porch and roof overhang shield the windows from the blazing sun and monsoon-like rains. Another typical coastal feature cannot be seen: behind the ground-level latticework are pilings to elevate the structure. Only a stone's throw from the town waterfront, the Cotter house had no protection whatsoever from the 1919 hurricane. The swept-back pilings are all that remained of the house. They are mute testimony to the tremendous power of an onrushing storm surge.

The August 1942 storm slammed ashore when the military was building facilities to defend the Aransas Pass from German submarines. This photograph of the storm flood was taken atop the U.S. Coast Guard station. The long building immediately behind the radio antenna is a recently constructed troop barrack. All military construction was halted until the end of hurricane season.

After the Civil War, Mustang Island became rangeland for a thriving cattle industry. When that industry petered out in the 1870s, the Island was left with many maverick cattle and a number of them drowned in the 1942 storm. Here a bloated bovine is inspected by GIs, two of whom hold their noses against the ghastly odor.

This is a 1942 storm view of "the Flats," the name of the commercial area close to the waterfront. Marine fuel depots and gas stations, like the Gulf station, presented a particular problem when their storage tanks leaked into the storm surge, adding the undesirable element of petroleum products to the floodwaters that invaded the town structures.

A hurricane can literally turn things topsy-turvy. These cottages once belonged to the Port Aransas Hunt Club of the 1920s. When the club dissolved, townsfolk bought the structures for various purposes, one being to create Island cottages. The 1942 storm did not spare this popular tourist facility.

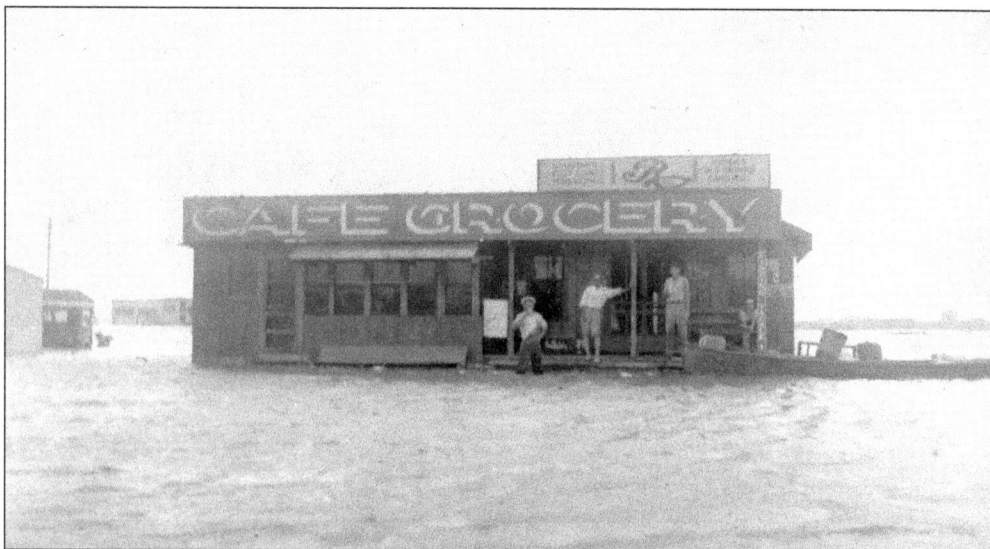

The typical after-storm behavior of Port Aransans is shown in this 1942 image. Little boats—one is tied up to the right of the building—replace cars and trucks. The men's casual postures and the consuming of what is no doubt beer, signal a "been there, done that" attitude about hurricanes.

Back when the town had two-digit telephone numbers, Lenoree and Boone Walker operated the Port Aransas telephone exchange from this house. The August 1945 hurricane took half the roof, giving the Walker place this swayback look. The fence kept the free-range cattle from trampling or grazing the flower beds.

Gail Borden Munsill, of the Borden dairy dynasty, took an interest in Port A and invested in its development. Indeed, the first Port Aransas mall, which is shown here, was financed by Munsill in the 1920s. The 10 storefronts indicate that the mall was built to be a busy place—the space to the far right was a laundry. A hurricane can utterly destroy people's hopes and dreams. The image below shows the Munsill mall after the 1945 storm.

Post Office - Port Aransas, Texas   6-L-399

Next to the post office in 1961 was Gaulding's Port Aransas Mercantile, the town grocery, which is now the Souvenir City store. The above photograph of Gaulding's, notably with its walls intact, was taken right before Hurricane Carla. The other image of Gaulding's speaks to a psychological characteristic of post-storm Port Aransas. Even though the wall of the grocery and much of its roof are gone, the shelves have been neatly restacked, sending the inspiring message, "business as usual." Carla was the fifth major hurricane to hit Port A.

In August 1970, Hurricane Celia was an even bigger storm than Carla. A strong storm surge was accompanied by ferocious winds, some gusts exceeding 170 miles per hour. These two unique photographs were taken in the calm of Celia's eye. What looks like a river scene is actually Port A's main drag, Alister Street. The waist-deep wader among the buildings is Frank Gibbs, owner of the popular Gibbs Cottages motor court. What is discouraging about the eye of the storm is that its calmness is just the prelude to the next—and often more intense—phase of the hurricane.

Celia, the last major hurricane to strike Port Aransas, damaged yet another popular tourist facility, the Seahorse Lodge. It was repaired and today is still at the corner of Avenue G and Trojan Street.

Of course, commercial structures were not the only places destroyed by Celia. This is a home in the Port Aransas Private Marina, a community of weekend houses built on little boat canals next to the Aransas Pass waterway. That location meant these structures took the brunt of both Celia's winds and waves, although this particular house appears to have been laid waste by a tornado, another terror associated with hurricanes.

Hurricane Celia did not spare the fishing industry, a mainstay of the Port Aransas economy. Before the storm struck, the *Marlin Queen* party boat—"party" denotes many fishermen—took up to 25 people into the gulf to fish for tasty red snapper and grouper. Port Aransas is also the home port of private and charter boats of the sport fisherman—also known as deep-sea fishing—class of boats. The storm surge deposited this sport fisherman a quarter-mile from the marina. Only minimally damaged, the boat was refloated soon after this photograph was taken.

Three

THE ARÁNZAZU

The Spanish name for the waterway or pass between Mustang and San José Islands was Aránzazu, named after a holy place in Spain. Sometime in the 1830s, when Anglo-Americans were quickly settling in Texas, Aránzazu was Anglicized to the Aransas Pass.

Since 1836—the year of Texas's independence from Mexico—the Aransas Pass, which serves as a maritime route to various points of commerce, has been important to the economies of both Texas and the United States. Accordingly, the federal government decided in 1880 to make the natural pass safer for ships by building a jetty system.

There are two reasons this chapter was dedicated to the construction of the Aransas Pass jetties. Firstly, the building of the jetties is itself an engaging historical story, one that saw millions of tons of rocks cleverly managed and transformed into two massive jetty structures. Secondly, the building of the jetties was the historic event that began the transition of Port Aransas from a pioneer coastal village into a thriving tourist community. Here is an overview of how that happened.

As the jetty workmen, supervisors, and engineers labored at the watery Aransas Pass, they found it teeming with tarpon, a game fish highly valued by sport fishermen. Eager to go fishing, some of these men hired Mustang Islanders to row them out to the tarpon. Stories about the world-class tarpon fishing on Mustang Island circulated in the sport fishing world, and by the 1890s, fishermen were regularly arriving and hiring local guides. The Islanders began realizing that a whole economy could be achieved by attracting mainlanders, or tourists, to Mustang.

It was the tarpon that started Port Aransas on the road toward becoming a thriving tourist destination. Because it was the building of the Aransas Pass jetties that brought the tarpon to center stage, the Aránzazu story is fundamental to Port Aransas history.

This is a fine view of the Aransas Pass and its jetties. The straight south jetty at the left and the curved north jetty are attached, respectively, to the islands of Mustang and San José. In managing a pass, jetties accomplish three things. Most obviously, they calm the water by creating a lee and also keep silt from clogging the pass's ship channel. Less obviously, jetties maintain the depth of that channel by an effect called scouring, the directing of currents through the channel. The curved north jetty was the product of an engineer who thought curvature would increase jetty efficiency. He was proved wrong, but not in time to keep his jetty from being installed. The building of the Aransas Pass jetties is history that is interesting from both engineering and human perspectives.

A railroad and barge system was used to build the rock jetties (see map). Flatcars bearing rocks arrived in the town of Aransas Pass and were transferred to a rail line trestle going over Redfish Bay. This photograph shows flatcars on this trestle line, which terminated at a dock. When the railcars arrived there they were rolled onto barges, and the barges were pushed to receiving docks on Mustang and San José Islands (the white squares on the map). The jetties were built in stages, two funded by the federal government and the other funded by the Aransas Pass Harbor Company located in Aransas Pass.

The rocks used to build the jetties came from a quarry near San Antonio, Texas, about 150 miles from the coast. Jetty plans called for a hierarchical rock stratum—smallest rocks on the bottom progressively building up to the largest rocks. The San Antonio quarry and some rock-laden flatcars are shown here. These flatcars were hauled from San Antonio to the dock in Redfish Bay (see previous map). The photograph below shows an engine pushing flatcars onto the dock.

The above image is another view of the Redfish Bay dock. The tugboat is next to a barge with rails on it. The locomotive pushed the rock cars onto this barge, which was then pushed by tugboat down the barge route shown on the previous map. For building the north and south jetties, the rock barges landed at receiving docks located on San José and Mustang Islands. The image below is of the Mustang receiving dock.

Government Work at Port Aransas.

From each receiving dock, a trestle rail line was built into the Gulf of Mexico. The building of one of those lines is shown at left; a steam pile driver hammers down pilings that will support a trestle. Later, rails were laid atop the trestle. The other photograph shows rock cars on a trestle line going into the gulf. Workers are throwing rocks overboard. It was tedious dumping enough rocks to make the two large jetties. The job lasted from 1895 to 1919.

The final stage of the jetty building involved laying capstones and channel dredging. Each jetty was capped by huge pieces of pink granite from a quarry near Austin, Texas. Pictured here is a flatcar with five capstone pieces, each weighing about eight tons. The other image is of a dredge boat that helped deepen the Aransas Pass ship channel located between the jetties.

Government Dredge at Aransas Harbor.

Oct. 13. 08

Jetty construction was overseen by the U.S. Army Corps of Engineers and the *c.* 1890 building shown above was the corps's headquarters at the Aransas Pass. The engineers building still stands today as a dormitory on the campus of the University of Texas Marine Science Institute, on the east side of Port Aransas. One person who spent time in the engineers building was D. M. Picton, shown at left. He was the owner of the construction company that won the government contract to build the north and south jetties. Picton, in partnership with J. P. Nelson, also built the railroad line over Redfish Bay that was so crucial to the constructing of the jetties.

Some of the jetty workers were immigrants. The gentleman pictured here, Matteo Bujan, hailed from Croatia. Bujan eventually settled in Port Aransas and his grandson Charles currently serves on the city council. An interesting story associated with the jetty labor force is that a town ordinance prohibited saloons from serving "foreigners." That prejudicial policy did not sit well with a man who was fresh from Europe, Tomas Jakasovitch. He Anglicized his name to Thomas Mathews and responded to the discriminatory ordinance by building a floating saloon—the ordinance had no authority offshore. The only requirement at Tom Mathews' Deep Water Saloon, pictured below around 1909, was that a man had enough money to pay his bar tab.

Pictured above is the construction of a seaport warehouse, and below is a cargo ship docked at the completed port. These pictures, from around 1911, represent an economic consequence of the Aransas Pass waterway being made safe for shipping by the jetty system described above. The jetties made the pass navigable so that shipping lines began using the pass without fear of losing their vessels' unpredictable currents and variable depths. The seaport was on Harbor Island, immediately west of Port Aransas. This port was for the export of Texas cotton to the clothing mills of Europe; the docked ship is an English freighter. The Harbor Island cotton port provided many jobs for Port Aransas townsfolk until it closed in 1926. The loss of the maritime economy that year motivated Port Aransans to seek out a new economy—the commitment to a full-time tourist industry.

The Harbor Island cotton port was quite a significant event on the Texas coast. Companies and businesses in support of this port sprung up in the mainland town of Aransas Pass, 6 miles west of Harbor Island. One company dredged a small ship channel between Aransas Pass and the Harbor Island seaport. Barges stacked with bales of cotton were pushed down the Aransas Channel to the port. The above image is of a boatload of well-wishers at the opening of this channel in 1911. The image below is a throng of well-wishers at the gala opening of the Harbor Island seaport in 1912.

Fishing for Spanish Mackerel on South Jetty, Port Aransas, Tex.

Another result of the jetties has nothing to do with maritime commerce and financial gain and everything to do with just plain fun and relaxation. The jetties are a favorite place to catch some rays, breathe the fresh gulf air, take a walk, have a picnic, propose marriage, get hitched, contemplate, daydream, meditate, practice yoga, write poetry, compose music, paint, take photographs, scuba dive, people and boat watch, and last—but certainly far from least—the jetties are a great place to go fishing. Scenes like this one from the 1920s still happen most days in the summertime.

Four

LIVELIHOODS

As a vacation destination, Port Aransas naturally has jobs in the tourist industry. Tourism, however, did not become the primary economy until the late 1920s, and prior to that time, islanders engaged in far different livelihoods.

Surprisingly, Mustang Island's very first economy had nothing to do with "island" things like boats and fishing. After the Civil War, the Islanders were part of the booming South Texas cattle industry, which saw the shipping of beeves to northern markets.

The town names "Tarpon" and "Port Aransas" are telling markers in the history of livelihoods. World-class tarpon fishing was revealed in the 1880s and sport fishermen from near and far began descending on the Island. The fishing guide business took off, and in 1896 people named their community "Tarpon" in honor of its finned benefactor.

In 1912, a seaport opened on nearby Harbor Island and the people of Tarpon found good maritime jobs there. In celebration of that bounty, the townsfolk changed their town name from Tarpon to Port Aransas to show their commitment to the town's maritime economy over its sport fishing industry. A series of events closed the Harbor Island seaport in 1926, precipitously ending Port A's maritime economy. The townsfolk relied on sport fishing to keep the wolf from the door while they worked to establish a broader tourist industry that appealed to more than just fishermen. This is the topic of the next chapter.

Compiling materials about the history of livelihoods revealed two things about Port Aransans and work. People did not hesitate to hold more than one job. One such person managed a motor court, kept the books for her husband's fishing guide business, and decorated seashells to sell at a souvenir shop. Secondly, there was great team play on the Island. Being a self-reliant group of people, the islanders tackled a myriad of jobs that required large numbers of people to work together in smooth and efficient ways. These admirable work characteristics are still evident in the people of Port Aransas.

During the Civil War, the North depleted its cattle herds by feeding and clothing large armies. That meant that after the war, cattle-rich south Texas was in a prime position to supply the hungry Northern marketplace. Having plentiful grass, a shallow water table, and a natural fence courtesy of the gulf and bay, Mustang Island was good cow country. This image of the calf and her white pelican neighbors harkens back to the days of the Mustang cattle industry, roughly from 1866 to 1875. Beeves were boated to the slaughter and packing plant at nearby Rockport, shown in this illustration. From there, cattle and cattle products—tallow, hides, and bones—were shipped to Northern markets. (Below, courtesy of Corpus Christi Public Library.)

Commercial shipping provided significant livelihoods. After Mustang Island was settled in 1855, some islanders were in the lightering business. The model in this image is of a coastal lighter, a shallow draft boat about 25 feet in length. Large cargo ships could not sail the shallow water to Corpus Christi because there was not a ship channel to Corpus until 1926. Therefore, after ships came through the Aransas Pass, their cargoes were transferred to lighters for the shallow Corpus run. The warehouse and docked freighters were photographed from Harbor Island. The seaport, which operated from 1912 to 1926, exported Texas cotton and was an oil depot that provided Port Aransans jobs as stevedores, tugboat crewmen, and pressmen at the cotton press.

Bird's Eye View of Docks and Warehouse, Aransas Pass, Tex.

Today Harbor Island still provides some Port Aransans with jobs. The above image is of a facility for servicing the offshore natural gas and petroleum industry. Service boats leave this dockage daily to take workers and supplies to gas and oil rigs in the Gulf of Mexico. The petroleum industry also provides livelihoods in terms of the marine transportation of various products. The image below shows a tugboat pushing a cargo of liquefied petroleum gas. Port Aransans work aboard these vessels that ply the extensive Intracoastal Waterway.

Port Aransans have commonly found work building boats. In 1918, the MacDonald shipbuilding yard opened on Harbor Island. This shipbuilder specialized in tanker ships, the new marine technology for transporting crude oil to gasoline refineries. The MacDonald tankers, one shown above, used concrete tanks, which prevented contamination of the oil by the rust and corrosion that came with metal tanks. This shipyard was destroyed by the 1919 hurricane. In 1915, Fred Farley began building boats for Port Aransas fishing guides and good woodworkers could find work at the Farley yard. In the image below, a worker prepares to install a cabin door. It was aboard a Farley boat that President Roosevelt fished for tarpon in 1937. The Farley operation closed in 1976.

Another marine livelihood involves the Aransas Pass. Transiting the pass requires a person who knows it well. Historically that person is an Aransas ship pilot. The pilot joins the captain to advise him in taking his ship through the pass. (Piloting was an early vocation on Mustang Island; both John and Edward Mercer were Aransas pilots.) The little sailboat pictured at left was the Aransas pilot boat around 1915. It took the pilot to the ship that he was to guide through the pass. The image below is today's Aransas pilot boat. The diagonal structure is what's known as the "Jacob's ladder." The pilot boat runs alongside the ship and the pilot uses that ladder to go onto and off of the ship. The ship does not slow down for this human transfer, so there is absolutely no room for error.

Not surprisingly, the water has provided numerous careers. The shallow bays around Port Aransas are home to tens of thousands of ducks during the winter months. When wild duck was a standard American table food, Port Aransans engaged in "market hunting," the commercial harvesting of waterfowl. This image shows a market hunter with his daily production, c. 1900. To prevent the extinction of waterfowl, market hunting was outlawed in 1905.

Commercial fishing once thrived in Port Aransas. This 1920s image shows commercial fishermen working a seine net—a net with floats at the top and held down by weights on the bottom. They walked the net out into a calm surf. After a time, the fishermen gathered the ends of the net together and used their vehicle to pull the net, hopefully full of fish, onto the beach.

A Catch of Red-Fish, Port Aransas, Tex.

Commercial fishing was also done by trotline. A trotline is a long line supported by floats. Attached to the line are baited hooks. After it had been out for a while, the fisherman went down the trotline—trotted the line—to remove fish and replenish baits. Commercial trotlining was once the way trout and redfish were caught in area bays. It is now illegal. This 1913 image is of two trotliners with a fine catch of redfish. The waterfront image, from around 1935, is of a Port A facility where fish were processed for shipment to the marketplace. Large commercial fishing operations on the mainland eventually ended Port A's mom-and-pop fishing businesses.

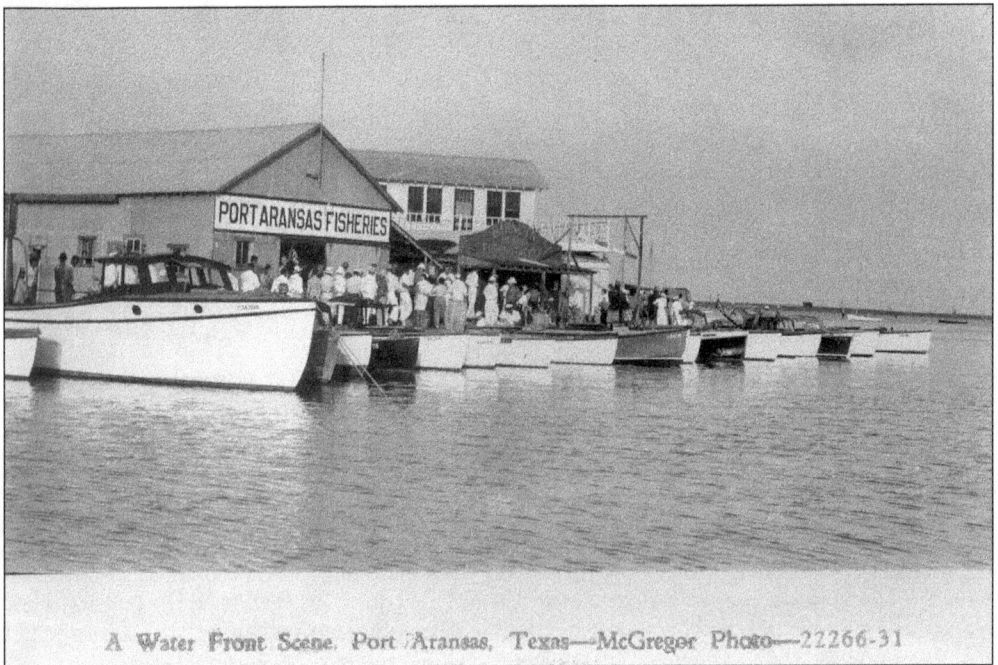
A Water Front Scene. Port Aransas, Texas—McGregor Photo—22266-31

In the later part of the 19th century, Port Aransas had a thriving business in the catching and exporting of turtles to restaurant marketplaces; at the time, turtle was prime table fare. Turtles were heavily concentrated in area waters, which may have been an offshoot of the cattle industry. When cattle were butchered for their tallow and hides, there was no way to preserve the meat. It was simply thrown into the water, providing an abundant food supply for turtles. This inverted turtle shows how the animals were immobilized for live shipment.

"TURTLE SOUP"
PORT ARANSAS, TEX.

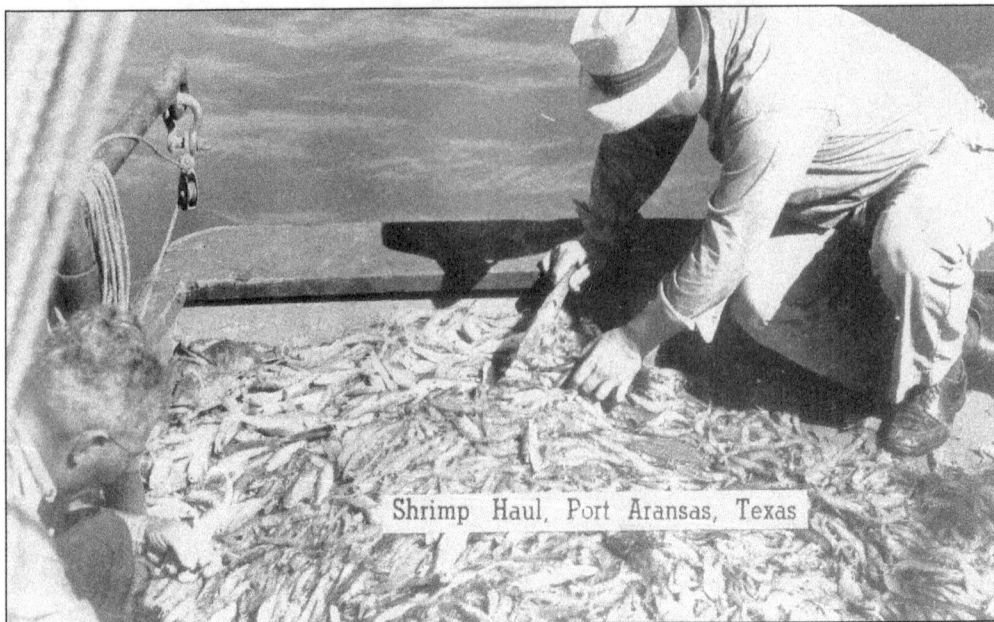

Shrimp Haul, Port Aransas, Texas

Texas coastal shrimping has two domains: bay shrimping and offshore, or gulf, shrimping. For a time, Port Aransas had an offshore shrimping industry, as evidenced by this 1930s image of a Port Aransas shrimper culling through his catch. Today the town has only two offshore shrimp boats since the offshore shrimping industry moved to the town of Aransas Pass. One boat is the *Polly Anna*, seen below at her Port A moorings. Remarkably this beautiful 100-foot vessel was built by a Port Aransan on his residential property. People keep a close eye on *Polly Anna*. When she is away from dock it means that fresh shrimp—sold right off the boat—will be available the next day.

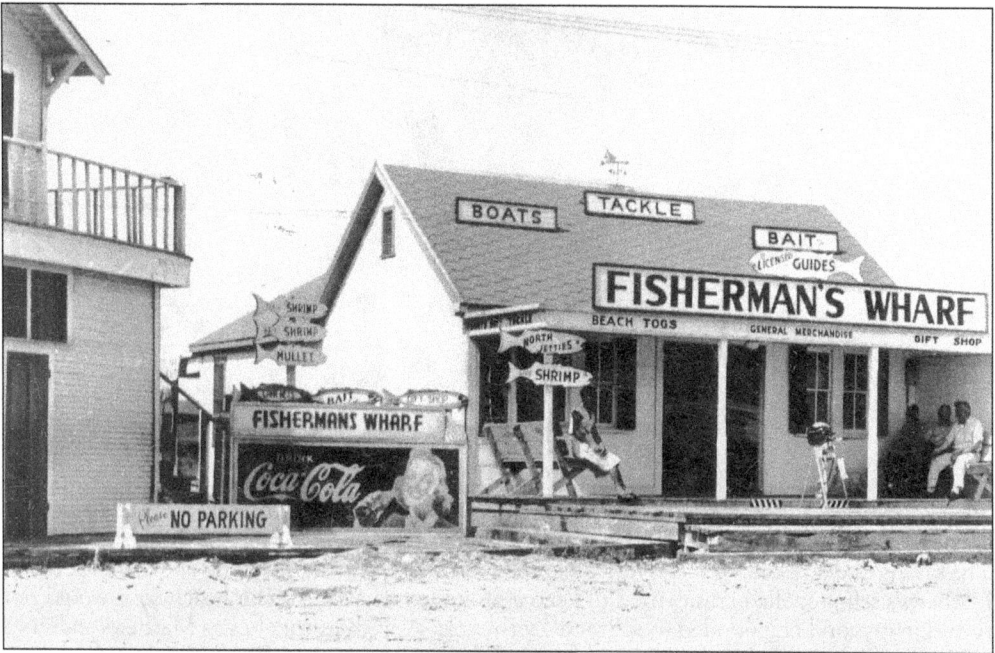

These are images of two iconic Port Aransas establishments: Fisherman's Wharf (in the 1950s) and Woody's (in the 1970s), both of which have since been modernized. These sport fishing places belong in this chapter because they are major outlets for Port Aransas bay shrimpers. Bay shrimp are used for baiting fishhooks. Additionally Woody's and Fisherman's Wharf sell sport fishing equipment and are headquarters for a number of bay guides and offshore charter captains. A visit to these stores—which both have dockside lounging areas ideal for beer sipping—gives one a sense of how integral fishing is to the town.

These homemade machines, both photographed in 1955, show the resourcefulness of Port Aransans. The saving of distressed vessels is fundamental in a coastal community. The above image is Ted Mathews's self-propelled crane, used to keep a grounded boat facing the beach so it would not turn sideways and be pounded to splinters by the surf. A woman watches as Mathews stabilizes her husband's grounded shrimp boat and waits for the high tide to refloat it. Melvin Littleton's 16-foot-high, balloon tire "Spider" was wholly unique. Spider was driven out into the surf and parked behind the grounded boat in deeper water. It then winched the boat toward it—and deeper water—until the boat's propeller could get a sufficient bite to power the boat out. Spider was anchored so it would winch itself toward the stranded vessel.

Five

THE TOURISTS ARRIVE

From 1912 to 1926, the Port Aransas economy was based on revenues from sporting and maritime-based businesses. Sportsmen from the mainland came to fish for tarpon and hunt ducks, and some townsfolk found work guiding these sporting tourists in those activities. However, the greater revenue during this time came from maritime jobs at the nearby seaport on Harbor Island (see page 45, bottom image). Townsfolk worked as stevedores, pressmen at the cotton press, and tugboat crewmen.

In 1926, the bigger and better Port of Corpus Christi opened. This neighboring port took so much business away from the Harbor Island seaport that it was forced to close, thus ending Port Aransas's maritime-based economy. To make up for that serious shortfall, the townsfolk had to expand the tourist trade beyond attracting only sportsmen. The town's economic survival depended on bringing in the larger family trade, but there was a problem.

At the start of 1926, there was no easy way for vehicles to get to Mustang Island from the mainland. Vehicular inaccessibility was not a particular problem for the visiting fishermen and hunters. They simply got to the Island aboard work scows or little pedestrian ferries. Those modes of transportation, however, were not family friendly. A man could not be expected to take his wife and children aboard a boat full of hootin' and hollerin' good old boys heading to Port Aransas to fish and party.

What was needed to attract families to Port A was a way for them to arrive on Mustang Island in the comfort and security of the family car. Until an expedient way was found to get vehicles onto the Island, there would be little, if any, family trade. And without that trade, the town would not be able to grow its tourist economy. At the start of 1926, the economic well-being of Port Aransas hung in the balance.

The vehicular inaccessibility problem was solved, and families began streaming into Port Aransas. The full-spectrum tourist industry became a reality, and the town was saved.

Vehicular access to Mustang Island (and hence Port Aransas) coincided with the 1926 closing of the cotton-exporting seaport on Harbor Island, which was a result of competition from the larger port of Corpus Christi. The closing of the Harbor Island facility meant lost revenue for the Aransas Harbor Terminal Railroad, which had carried cotton to the port. With no more cotton to haul, the railroad owners devised a way to make up for the lost revenue. Tourists, notably families, wanting to reach Mustang Island paid a toll to drive their vehicles onto the railroad's flatcars at the town of Aransas Pass. These "piggyback" flatcars were then pulled to Harbor Island. Once there, the tourists drove their vehicles off the train and onto the *Mitzi* ferry for a short ride over to Port Aransas. By providing easy access to the Island, particularly for families, the piggyback railroad and *Mitzi* were crucial keys to advancing the tourist industry in Port A. The piggyback railroad was replaced in 1931 when an asphalt vehicular roadway was laid over the rail bed.

The piggyback and ferryboat gave access to north Mustang Island but they did not benefit potential tourists from the mainland city of Corpus Christi, which is across from south Mustang Island. In 1928, that problem was solved by the Don Patricio Causeway. Troughs for car wheels were supported by trestles all the way from the mainland to Padre Island, just south of Mustang. Upon reaching Padre, people crossed to Mustang Island via a little bridge and then drove on the hard sand for 17 miles to Port Aransas. A popular weekend recreation was to reach Port A by the Don Patricio and beach drive, eat lunch at the Tarpon Inn, and then take the *Mitzi* ferry and the piggyback railroad back to the mainland; Corpus folks called this "making the circle." The Don Patricio Causeway was destroyed by a 1933 hurricane and not replaced by a modern roadway until 1950.

Vehicles are not the only way to reach Port Aransas. Several hundred visitors arrive each year by sailing right down the Aransas Pass. The Harvest Moon Regatta is a sailboat race from Galveston to Port Aransas that is sponsored by the Lakewood Yacht Club of Houston, Texas. Begun in 1987, the Harvest Moon is held in October, traditionally the best month for sailing Texas offshore waters. The regatta entails weekend sailors arriving to throw some of the biggest bashes the town sees all year. On the other hand, if air travel is more to one's liking, the Mustang Beach Airport is on the south edge of town. The airport has a 3,500-foot runway and self-serve Avgas fuel. To the right of the runway is the prestigious Island Moorings canal community developed in the 1980s.

In the early days, tourist lodging was provided by motor courts. In Port Aransas, that facility was—and still is to a great extent—a group of cottages, many having kitchen amenities. One of the classic motor courts, conveniently located two blocks from the beach, is the Gulf Beach Cottages, pictured here around 1960. It is still in operation. The first Port Aransas condominium was constructed in 1965. It ushered in the investment-minded tourists who were interested in purchasing a condo, enjoying it for a few weeks in the summer and then leasing it the remainder of the year. The condominium complex shown here is typical of the layout of many Port A condominiums.

Some tourists bring their lodgings with them. The above image, from around 1933, is (to the knowledge of the author) the first trailer facility in Port Aransas, located just off the beach half, a mile south of the jetty. Today Port A has numerous trailer and RV parks. One of the largest and best appointed is Pioneer Park. Three rigs are shown here parked by an attractive freshwater pond. Pioneer Park is particularly popular with winter visitors from the North, the majority hailing from Minnesota. Although some come before Christmas, most winter folks arrive in January and stay until mid-March, which is the start of the frenetic spring break period.

While sport fishing and beach going are now magnets for the Port Aransas tourist trade, there was a time when mainlanders came to town to engage in less wholesome activities. After World War II, Port A had a distinctly honky-tonk ambiance, particularly in the area by the waterfront known as the "Flats." There were saloons and clubs, some of which had illegal gambling and more. While La Balenise Room saloon was surely a legitimate place, it is illustrative of the 1950s Flats. This guest card was handed out upon showing proof of age and paying a cover charge. In 1961, Hurricane Carla literally blew and washed away the honky-tonk era. When Port Aransas was rebuilt, the townsfolk focused on creating a family-centered community, and they definitely succeeded.

GUEST CARD   GUEST CARD

LA BALENISE ROOM

PORT ARANSAS   PHONE 77

(OVER)

Part and parcel of a tourist town, particularly one that is family oriented, is the souvenir shop. Prior to Hurricane Celia in 1970, the structure shown here was the Port Aransas Mercantile, a general store with roots back to the 1920s. The structure survived the storm, but owners Sam and Bea Allen decided not to continue the business. They sold the building to Bob Clark, who in 1973 opened Souvenir City, Port A's first dedicated "shell shop"—a moniker reflecting the many seashell products sold there, along with other popular items like t-shirts and beachwear and supplies. Today Souvenir City is at the same location on Alister Street and looks very much as it did when it opened.

The next Port A shell shop was the Islander, which opened in 1982 and was renovated in 2003. Its lighthouse was motivated by the famous Lydia Ann Lighthouse that lies a mile north of Port Aransas. The Islander's distinctly painted lighthouse and six multicolored sea horses have achieved iconic status on Alister Street.

White Marlin Porpoise Circus
Port Aransas, Texas

Featuring bottlenose dolphins from local waters, the White Marlin Porpoise Circus was a favorite tourist attraction in the 1960s. The show was part of White Marlin Enterprises, which was begun by Ralph Plumlee in 1964. White Marlin contributed significantly to the tourist industry by adding motels, a restaurant, and a party fishing boat. White Marlin Enterprises ceased operations soon after the 1970 hurricane.

Port Aransas recently added an ecotourism feature. Taking full advantage of being the "birdiest small coastal community in America"—dubbed so because of its more than 185 species—the town built the Leonabelle Turnbull Birding Center in 1994. The overwater boardwalk and observation tower are in a backwater area that permits undisturbed viewing and scenic photographic contexts. The birding center, reached by walking alongside a garden of indigenous flowers and plants, is a reason that Port A is a red letter stop on the Great Texas Coastal Birding Trail. The trail goes from the Louisiana border, down the coast, then up the Rio Grande River to Laredo.

THE GREAT TEXAS
COASTAL BIRDING
TRAIL

80 Reasons To Stay Away From the Alligators

There is more to the Leonabelle Turnbull Birding Center than just fine, feathered friends. As this sign at the entrance to the boardwalk informs, the center is also home to at least two alligators, with 13-foot-long Boots being the sentimental favorite. The number 80 refers to the number of gator teeth appearing in the sign.

When the wind picks up, the Gulf of Mexico surf can be a bit much for young children. In that event, an excellent back-up plan is to take the family to the beautiful community park swimming pool, which opened in 1999. For those interested in exercise, the park also has a pet-friendly jogging and walking track.

Developed in the late 1990s, the Beachwalk community of single-family dwellings marks an economic and social landmark for Port Aransas. The community is comprised of mainlanders who have chosen Port A not as a transient weekend or vacation spot, but as their life destination. The community is not on the water per se. The water in this image is one of several man-made ponds within the community. A variant on the Beachwalk theme is currently being developed. Cinnamon Shores will incorporate service and retail establishments, making it a partially self-contained community, a first on Mustang Island. The traditional tourist model is now being supplemented by the destination model, which will appreciably increase the residential population of Mustang Island in the ensuing decades.

Six

SAND, SUN, AND SURF

One way to discover why people come to Port Aransas is to observe the vehicles waiting in line at the summertime ferry landing. Various contractors' trucks are on their way to the many job sites in town, and the staples in the big food service trailers will be unloaded at convenience stores and restaurants. The recreational vehicles are going to parks where their owners will enjoy the company of like-minded travelers. Jetty fishermen are known by their rods protruding out car windows or in holders mounted on the bumper, and the fishermen heading to the Gulf of Mexico or bays are evident by the boats they have in tow.

A great number of vehicles in the ferry line are transporting America's most valuable cargo: mom, dad, and the kids. Perhaps they are thinking about fishing, shopping, and the seafood meals just across the ship channel. Nevertheless, it is a good bet that what summertime families are most anticipating is time at the beach. Such is often clearly spelled out on the SUV windows: Port "A" Beach or Bust!

The first tourists in Port Aransas were not beachgoers; they were sport fishermen focused on landing good-sized tarpon. But as Mustang Island became more and more accessible to vehicular traffic, more and more families started coming to Port Aransas. While dad was enjoying his sporting activities, it was natural for mom and the children to go to the beach to look for seashells, frolic in the surf, and build sand castles.

While Port Aransas is certainly still a fishing destination, make no mistake about where most visitors spend their time, a fact readily revealed by a drive on the summertime beach.

A vista of the gulf side of Mustang Island is shown in this 1930s photograph. Port A's main street is three blocks from the beach. The wide beach gives way to the rolling sand dunes of this barrier island. The seven Texas barrier islands are relative newcomers in the geological world. Starting as submerged shoals, the islands broke the surface about 3,500 years ago and soon acquired the general configurations we see today. With the advent of cars came the Texas tradition of beach driving. That is sometimes challenged by developers seeking to disallow vehicles on the beach next to their hotels or housing developments, but such action invariably fails. In fact, a movement is underway to protect vehicular right-of-way on public beaches by an amendment to the state constitution.

Port Aransas contributes to positive family moments. It is commonplace for people to revisit—and even move to—Port A based on childhood memories. Many such memories are associated with the beach. This classic 1950s image shows a multigenerational family eager to enjoy the Port Aransas sun and surf. The girl at the right is ready to preserve memories with her Brownie camera while the fellow behind her, perhaps her granddad, looks out from under his Panama-style chapeau. The beach is not without its characters, one of whom is shown below. In his war surplus jeep, Salty Johns was a Port A goodwill ambassador who charmed many beachgoers in the 1950s and 1960s. Salty is remembered telling ghost stories around a roaring beach fire. The little dog, Junior, was himself quite a showman.

The Port Aransas beach has always been blessed by folks ready to share the latest in fashionable beachwear. Marion Fersing, a longtime resident of Port Aransas, sits atop a 1951 Ford sporting beach attire and a jaunty straw hat. The four women below, arms akimbo, model the latest in 1920s bathing costumes. The long shadows show their day on the Port A beach is coming to a close.

Feeding the gulls is a beach tradition. Called "sky rats" by the locals, the omnivore gulls are always looking for food. Gull feeding is frowned upon where their droppings have an undesirable consequence, such as on ferryboats where immobile cars are vulnerable under a cloud of pooping gulls. The predominant gull on the Port A beach is the laughing gull, *Leucophaeus atricilla*. This bird takes three years to acquire its adult plumage and in the winter loses its black hood.

The beach is a place of discovery and finding seashells is a timeless favorite activity. The Port A beach has 18 different types of shells, and the particularly popular ones are shown in this image. The little oblong lettered olive is followed (clockwise) by a sand dollar, an Atlantic bay scallop with an Atlantic cockle next to it, another sand dollar, and a pair of lightning whelks, the Texas state shell. Sand dollars are actually skeletons of a bottom-dwelling animal. The spaghetti-like material in the photograph is soft coral. The 1912 image below shows a youngster with his discovery of a beached bottlenose dolphin. While dolphins are known to swim onto the beach and become stranded, this was an old animal that simply expired and washed ashore.

Just off the beach are the Mustang Island sand dunes. These rolling hills of shining sand and dark shadows provoke one to imagine mysterious forces and things concealed. Not surprisingly, the dunes play into Island myths and legends. Pirate Jean Lafitte buried treasure in the sand hills, marking the spot with a pistol impaled on an iron stake. And in 1885, a Mustang Islander, looking for a lost calf, spied the corner of an object protruding from a large dune. It was a strongbox of American and European gold pieces. The man used the windfall to become a wealthy south Texas real estate investor. The dunes also conceal treasures of actual history. An 1863 U.S. Navy antimine raft was discovered in 1980 and later researched by an archeological team. The exact location of this piece of Americana remains a closely guarded secret.

On a stretch of salt grass 100 yards behind the beach, two youths discovered, around 1948, a Skyraider naval aircraft that had crash landed. One of the boys climbed into the cockpit to give a thumbs-up for this intriguing discovery and perhaps to his dream of someday becoming a naval aviator.

The beach is a place of creativity, particularly in terms of building sand castles. And there are sand castles extraordinaire on the Port Aransas beach during the annual Sand Fest. Started in 1998, Sand Fest is an international sand-sculpting competition. This aerial shot is of Sand Fest 2009. In addition to professional sand sculpting, the event has children's classes about building sand castles and a myriad of vendors selling refreshments and a variety of merchandise. What the skilled Sand Fest competitors can do with sand is amazing, as shown by the intricate details of this dragon and tower sculpture.

The beach is a place to celebrate. Love and wellness are often celebrated on the Port A beach by marriage ceremonies and walking marathons. The images on this page show celebration of the spirit. This 1960s pastor, accompanied by a guitar, has brought some of his flock to the dunes to reflect upon and celebrate matters of the spirit. The shoeless couple in this 1937 photograph is having a jolly time celebrating another meaning of the word spirit. (Now there is an ordinance against having glass containers on the beach.)

Spring break is the biggest—and raunchiest—celebration on the Port Aransas beach. Over the decades, students from numerous colleges and high schools have flocked to Port A to party hardy during the famous March recess. The starting point of the great beach bash is sometimes the Dunes condominium, the tall structure in the background of the above image. The meeting, greeting, and imbibing shown in these images continues down the packed beach for what the breakers call the "Misery Mile," in reference to how they feel "the morning after."

LIFE'S A BEACH

The Port A beach is popular with Texas surfers. Surfing caught on in Port Aransas in the early 1960s, and soon wave riders were staging contests to hone their skills. The above image is of a competition held close to the Horace Caldwell pier in 1967. This structure is a favorite surfing venue because it is located in the area of relatively high surf, made even better for surfing by storms. The below image, taken from the pier, shows large waves pushed in by a storm churning through the Gulf of Mexico. During mandatory hurricane evacuation, die-hard surfers are among the last to leave Mustang Island. (Above, courtesy of Larry Haas.)

The dunes, locally called "sand hills," teem with fauna and flora. Skyward-reaching sea oats, ground-hugging goat's foot morning glories, and coastal bluestem grass hold down the sand, thus preserving the dunes. Sand hills are home to rattlesnakes, coyotes, jackrabbits, and kangaroo rats that are capable of living with practically no water. These 1920s cars below reached the beach from the west side of the Island on little roads that were once cow paths meandering through the dunes; these have since been converted to hard-surface beach access roads. When the condominium era started in the 1960s, several condos were built atop the dunes. Thankfully an ordinance protecting the dunes was put in place by the City of Port Aransas in 1975.

Sometimes the Port Aransas beach is anything but fun. Gulf storms or mechanical malfunctions can ground vessels in the blink of an eye. These 1950s images show shrimp boats aground in the surf line. In the above image, coastguardsmen use a rescue boat to bring in the captain of the disabled shrimper. In the other image, conditions have necessitated removing a crew member using a breeches buoy. This device is a canvas seat suspended under a life preserver. The seat is attached to a line running from the distressed vessel to a rescue platform, in this case a vehicle with a winch mechanism.

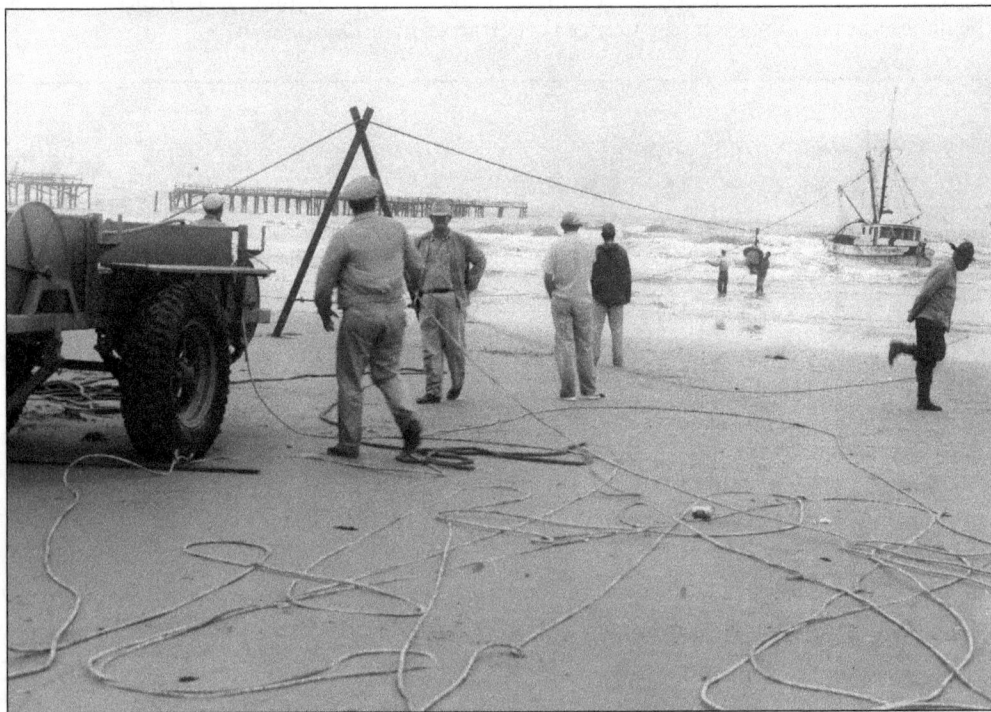

Seven

FISHING VENUES

More images in this book are dedicated to fishing than to any other topic, and so it should be. Not only is fishing integral to the fabric of Mustang Island and Port Aransas, it was fishing that was greatly responsible for creating the fabric itself.

The fishing around Port Aransas is good because the town docks are only a short boat ride from four fish-rich bays that are amply sustained by the Aransas Pass. The big three bay game fish—flounder, speckled trout, and redfish—inhabit Aransas, South, Redfish, and Corpus Christi bays, all of which are in close proximity to the pass. To understand how the Aransas Pass and the bays are linked, think of the pass as a lifeline to the Gulf of Mexico. The pass brings the incoming tide to the bays, then infuses it with the gulf's oxygenated and nutrient-rich water. The pass also benefits fishing in another way. The game fish migrate back and forth from the bays to the gulf, and for that, the Aransas Pass is a piscatorial super-highway.

As for offshore fishing, along Texas's coast, littoral currents sweep the gulf's blue water fairly close, and it is in the blue (versus green) water that numerous popular deep-sea game fish dwell, such as bill fish and tuna.

The importance of fishing to Mustang Island has led to some erroneous historical beliefs. For instance, many think that the first Island settlers in 1855, the Mercers, relied on fish and shrimp as a primary food source. But the Mercers, who were farmers and stockmen by trade, did not have the faintest idea how to fish, nor would they for some time. The Mercers did not have shrimp as a basic staple either because shrimp are bottom dwellers and could not be procured in quantity until the appearance of shrimp trawler boats in 1917. Even then it took Prohibition to elevate shrimp to an acceptable table fare in America. The little crustaceans, accompanied by a tangy sauce, were served in a "prohibited" cocktail glass, giving rise to the now famous shrimp cocktail.

It is ironic that the first recorded acknowledgment of Mustang Island's fabulous fishing involved a tiny, no-name slough. In 1875, a repairman was working at the area lighthouse, pictured here, and on his days off he fished a nearby slough. He wrote his wife, "Never seen so many fish. Catching them on every cast." A bit later he wrote, "No more fishing—too many of them. Can not stand to see any more fish."

uncle john —— his party.
john to granny Carston 1917

The next fishing venue was the Aransas Pass. Starting in the 1880s, men who were working on the jetties hired townsfolk to row them to fish the tarpon that populated the pass. Here is an image from 1917 or earlier of a guide and his party just off the partially completed south jetty. World-class tarpon fishing brought fishermen to Port Aransas and set it on the road to becoming a thriving tourist destination.

82

The jetties are arguably the most popular Port Aransas fishing venue because the submerged rocks provide the type of structure that attracts fish. Fishing the south jetty is an easy matter because it is attached to Mustang Island. To fish the north jetty, shown in this 1915 image, the Aransas Pass must first be crossed. That happens aboard a pedestrian ferry, appropriately named the *Jetty Boat*. Here the vessel is picking up fishermen from the north jetty loading dock. There is no ferry service after dark, so missing the last pick-up means spending the night on the jetty.

South jetty & pier
Port Aransas, Texas

Piers have always been popular fishing venues. Port Aransas has had three piers reaching into the Gulf of Mexico. The first one, called Jetty Pier, was an angled structure going out from the beach and then turning 90 degrees to connect to the south jetty. Wet and slimy rocks made the step from pier to jetty a challenging affair.

SOUTH PIER
PORT ARANSAS, TEX.

Jetty Pier had a rival named South Pier, which was located approximately where Avenue G currently intersects the beach. South Pier outlasted Jetty Pier, which closed in the 1930s.

84

South Pier was a boon during the Great Depression. Unable to afford to rent boats or have guides take them fishing, average folks enjoyed the pier as a fishing venue where they could wet a hook and socialize for less than a dollar. This image shows people having a great day pulling in black drum and redfish.

South Pier succumbed to battering waves in the 1950s and was replaced by another wood structure, the Horace Caldwell Pier. That pier was destroyed by storm waves in 1980 and was replaced by a reinforced concrete structure of the same name. This image is of the current Horace Caldwell Pier photographed from a quarter-mile offshore.

The beach offers surf fishing and the Port A surf has a feature that makes this fishing venue a productive one. Wading into the surf, one encounters depressions in the seabed called "guts." Surf fishermen like the guts because that is where the game fish are. The image at left, from around 1940, is noteworthy. The surf fisherman is Fr. Cyril Kuehne, a priest who wrote a Port Aransas history in 1977. The surf fishing image below is of a 7-foot-long shark caught in a gut only 20 yards from shore.

Rods in plastic holders represent the town's shore fishing venue. Port Aransas has a seawall-barricaded shoreline that runs from Roberts Point Park, shown in this image, to an area called Charlie's Pasture. Along this shoreline, a favorite fishing locale is next to the ferry landing. The constant turning of the ferryboat propellers disturbs the bottom, causing little fish and shrimp to be agitated. That activity brings in redfish, a favorite catch of the shore-fishing crowd.

This wade fisherman represents the bay fishing venue. Wading is popular in shallow bay flats because one can approach feeding game fish without spooking them. Wade fishing does, however, come with a cautionary note. Stepping down on a bottom-dwelling stingray can result in being stabbed by a sharp barb. To minimize that happening, wade fishermen shuffle their feet to nudge rays out of the way.

These images represent the offshore fishing venue. The above 1950s image is of a captain standing proudly aboard his new, all-wood charter boat. The equipment on the bulkhead to his left is a state-of-the-art, vacuum-tube marine radio, and the two aft-facing fighting chairs are ready for action. The below photograph shows a contemporary offshore fishing boat. Its fiberglass construction means far less maintenance and a longer hull life compared to wooden boats. The two tall, swept-back poles are outriggers, devices used in fishing for marlin and sailfish. The industry name for an offshore fishing boat like this one is "sport fisherman."

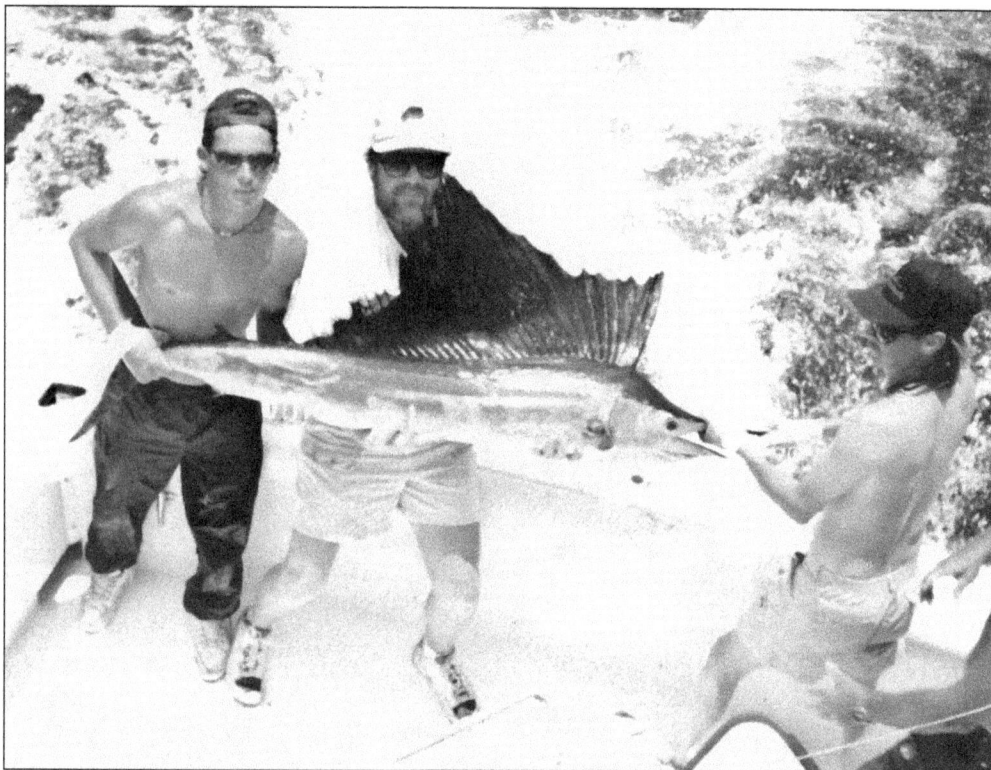

Aboard a sport fisherman, deckhands manage the bill and tail of a handsome sailfish while the fisherman holds the girth. Advances in the science of taxidermy mean that trophy fish like this one can now be photographed and released. Using synthetic materials, taxidermists can work from photographs to create mounts indistinguishable from the real thing that have much longer wall lives.

The *Dolphin Express* represents the other aspect of offshore fishing. A party boat, the *Dolphin Express* takes 25 people to oil and gas rigs. While a variety of fish feed by those structures, two of the most popular and delicious ones are the grouper, or sea bass, and red snapper. The typical party boat departs the Port A docks at 7 a.m. and returns at 4 p.m. If one is susceptible to motion sickness, a seasick preventive is strongly advised.

The privately owned outboard motorboat is itself a fishing venue. This 1960s image vividly shows the impact outboard motors had on the Port Aransas fishing business. One may note that there is not a Port A fishing guide on this boat. While the town initially spurned outboard motorboats for impacting that venerable business, the vast amount of gas, ice, bait, and beer bought by the outboard motorboat crowd soon eased the pain.

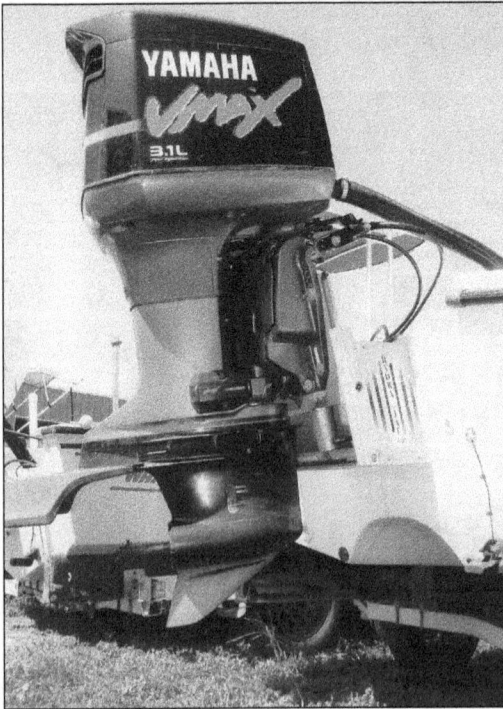

The fishing boat at left is not environmentally friendly. The entire engine (here the propeller is removed for repair) is elevated, and the keel of the boat is scooped out. Those features let this craft operate at full speed in water a foot deep, an operation which destroys delicate flora and scatters fish. To prevent that from happening, the state has designated "no prop zones" in which motors cannot be operated.

Eight

FISHING EVENTS

A tall fellow in his 20s walked casually into Barney's Place on the Port Aransas waterfront. The bespectacled storekeeper was busy behind the counter, so the potential customer took the opportunity to look around.

The floorboards creaked as he strolled over to the racks of fishing rods and shelves full of Penn fishing reels, equipment capable—given the nod from Lady Luck—of turning even the greenest amateur into a celebrated angler. But what really struck the man was the briny, waterfront smell of the place. This was just what he was looking for: a no-nonsense fishing establishment on waters known for their world-class tarpon fishing.

His business concluded, Barney adjusted his glasses and smiled at the man. "How can I help you?"

"I'm looking to do some tarpon fishing," the fellow answered as he walked over to the counter.

"Well, friend, you're in the right town and the right place for that," Barney grinned, opening the logbook which had the names and schedules of the tarpon guides. The men then worked out the particulars for a fishing trip.

Barney reviewed the entry and extended his hand, "I'm Barney Farley. And now all I need is your name for the log."

As the two fishing enthusiasts shook hands, the young man replied casually, "My name is Elliott, Elliott Roosevelt."

It was October 13, 1936, and some suspect young Roosevelt was on the Texas coast fish scouting for his famous father, Franklin. As much as Barney Farley might have been impressed that day, his experience was a pale shadow of how he would feel six months later when the yacht of the president of the United States steamed down the Aransas Pass.

An old-time Port Aransas angler once said, "Our big-time fishing makes for big-time things." The events in this chapter prove him right

The Aransas Pass is the birthplace of fishing on Mustang Island. In the 1880s, jetty workers paid some islanders, the original fishing guides, to take them to fish the thousands of tarpon that inhabited the pass. Word of Mustang Island's stellar fishing spread throughout the sport fishing community, eventually reaching the ears of Ned Green, a wealthy New Yorker. Green came and fished for the tarpon, soon returning to build the palatial structure shown here. Named Tarpon Club, it was on the tip of San José Island, just across the Aransas Pass from Mustang. This private club was comprised of 40 well-to-do sportsmen from all over the country. Members got to Tarpon Club by taking a train to Rockport and then on to San José in the boat shown below around 1900. Tarpon Club disbanded around 1904.

Before Ned Green came on the scene, the Mustang Island guides took parties fishing in rowboats (see page 82, bottom image). That conveyance was too slow for the high-drive Tarpon Club fishermen, so Green sent guide Ed Cotter to Chicago to learn about gasoline motorboats, which were a new marine technology at the time. Green then bought a power launch, operated by Cotter, comparable to the craft shown above. That event, which advanced the guide business, was a milestone in Port Aransas fishing history. In the image below, taken around 1905, cigar-smoking Cotter uses a powerboat to tow rowboats—like a string of ducklings—out for a day of fishing.

The next significant event in Port A's fishing history was the Farley and Sons Boat Works. Fred Farley was a master wood boat builder who moved to Port Aransas in 1915. Listening to his fishing customers describe what they wanted, Farley began turning out boats that were the finest fishing machines on the Texas coast—some argue even beyond that. Farley did not create technical marine architectural plans. As the customer described his boating needs, Farley sketched out the corresponding product on a piece of lumber and worked from that drawing. The above image shows a worker planking the hull of a Farley boat. The 1930s image below is of guides' row on the Port Aransas waterfront. All the craft are Farley boats—note the stern-facing fighting chairs on the first boat.

The Farley boat had notable marine features, one being its stability in choppy water conditions, which, given the traditionally high winds in the area, was often the case. The image above shows a Farley riding nicely in the choppy water of the Aransas Pass. Not all Farley products were fishing boats. In the 1920s, a wealthy customer, Gail Borden Munsill, ordered a speedboat from the Farley works. This image below shows this craft's sleek mahogany hull being finished in the Farley shop. Powered by a 12-cylinder automobile engine, Munsill's *Terrible Edith* was capable of making 65 miles per hour.

Despite the start of the Great Depression, the fishing guide and commercial fishing businesses were holding their own in the early 1930s. In addition to being fishermen, many of the townsfolk were also storekeepers, builders, contractors, motor court owners, filling station operators—essentially, the backbone of the community. In 1932, these people formed a civic organization called the Port Aransas Boatmen's Association. The group's mission was to enhance town life by meeting—financially and otherwise—significant community needs. The group image above is of the 1937 boatmen; the photograph below shows a major contribution made by this organization. The boatmen provided the labor force that built the community center in 1949 and to this day it remains the center of social life in Port Aransas.

Barney Farley and Grady Kinsolving, a Corpus Christi newspaper man, had a grand idea. After people caught their tarpon, the fish were displayed on the waterfront and the fishermen and guide told the stories of their catches. Farley and Kinsolving noted that fishermen were quite competitive, always proud to display the biggest fish, and that the general public enjoyed watching this show-and-tell fishing custom. Farley and Kinsolving decided to capitalize on these things by staging a competitive tarpon fishing tournament with the proceeds generated from entry fees given to the town coffers. The first Texas Tarpon Rodeo was held in 1932, and the fun began at the sound of Farley's revolver. That was the signal for the boats to speed away to secure desirable locations in the tarpon waters.

McGREGOR PHOTO

The Texas Tarpon Rodeo had several distinctions. For one, it was the first saltwater fishing tournament on the Texas coast. Another defining moment is documented in this photograph of Totsy Millican with her 6-foot and 2-inch-long tarpon—the second-largest tarpon in the competition. Her husband edged her out with a tad larger fish. Some men grumbled about women being permitted to participate in the competition, but Millican's tremendous catch proved that women could certainly handle the big action. The next three Texas Tarpon Rodeo winners were women. The competition quickly became the town event in which almost everyone, in one way or other, got involved. These five schoolgirls were rodeo princesses sometime during the 1950s

Townsfolk took notice when President Roosevelt's son Elliott was in Port Aransas in 1936 to fish for tarpon. This photograph shows that young Roosevelt, on the left, did quite well on the trip. While Elliott might have been in Texas to visit friends and fish, it is also possible that the president, an avid fisherman himself, had his son go to Port Aransas to check on what was touted as world-class tarpon fishing. Whatever motivated the president to come to Port A worked. On April 29, 1937, the Commander in Chief was piped aboard the destroyer USS *Moffett*, shown below. Sailing from New Orleans, the *Moffett* and its escort arrived two days later and anchored just off the Aransas Pass jetties.

The *Moffett* was escorted by the USS *Decatur*, the four-stack World War I–era destroyer pictured here. Aware that the president was coming, townsfolk kept an eye on the horizon. When the *Decatur* and *Moffett* arrived and were riding at anchor, binoculars were trained on them to see the action. What fishing guide Barney Farley saw distressed him: *Moffett* launched a motorboat and the occupants began fishing around the jetties. People panicked that the president had decided not to use Port Aransas guides on his fishing trip. But good news soon followed when FDR enlisted local fishing talent. The presidential yacht, the *Potomac*, shown below at anchor just south of the lighthouse, soon arrived, and the presidential party transferred from the *Moffett* to the *Potomac* for the remainder of the trip.

President's Yacht "Potomac"
Port Aransas, Texas
Compton

The president's fishing goal was simple: catch a respectable-sized tarpon. But FDR's luck was running thin. In the above image, the president, seated at the stern, looks up at the tarpon he just landed, which is held by Elliott Roosevelt. That tarpon, a 4-footer, was not what FDR was hoping for. Soon after that photograph was taken, a press boat came alongside and a reporter asked the president about his catch. The image below shows the president answering the reporter's question with a very recognizable hand signal.

PRESIDENT ROOSEVELT TELLS A FISH STORY

The Port A boatmen, the local term for fishing guides, who were supervising President Roosevelt discussed the small tarpon that he caught. The consensus was that the escorting press and secret service boats were riding too closely, scaring away the larger and smarter fish. The president ordered the escort craft to fall back. Soon afterward, the president hooked his "big" fish. This famous image shows boatman Barney Farley, with Elliott Roosevelt behind him, holding up the 77 pound, 5-foot, 1-inch tarpon. The boatman in dark glasses is Ted Mathews, owner of the Farley boat pictured. The press boats were waved in to capture the moment. Many of their photographs appeared in *Life* magazine.

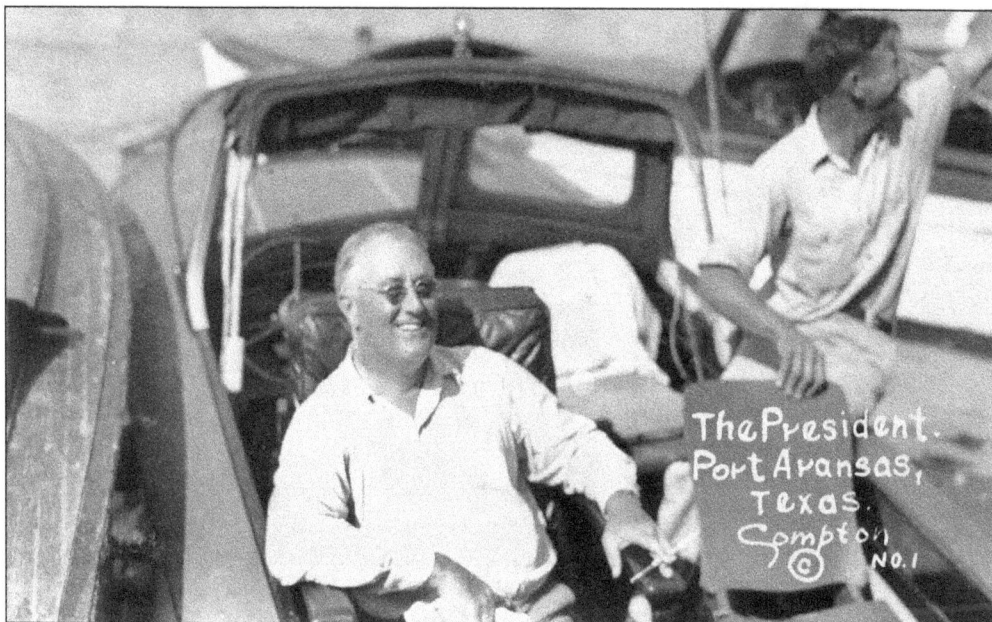

The President.
Port Aransas,
Texas.
Compton
© NO.1

Not surprisingly, President Roosevelt's visit created myths. It is not true that the president returned to Port Aransas for another tarpon trip, nor did he stay in Port A at the Tarpon Inn. In fact, Roosevelt never set foot on Mustang Island; he stayed aboard the *Potomac*. The closest he came to the Island was when his fishing boat docked at the Port A wharf so he could visit with townsfolk. The image above catches that moment. The fellow with the president is Ted Mathews. President Roosevelt did leave a lasting memento of his visit: a tarpon fishing custom called for people to sign a scale of the fish they caught, and the Tarpon Inn has a collection of 7,000 signed scales. The very special scale is the one bearing the signature of Franklin D. Roosevelt.

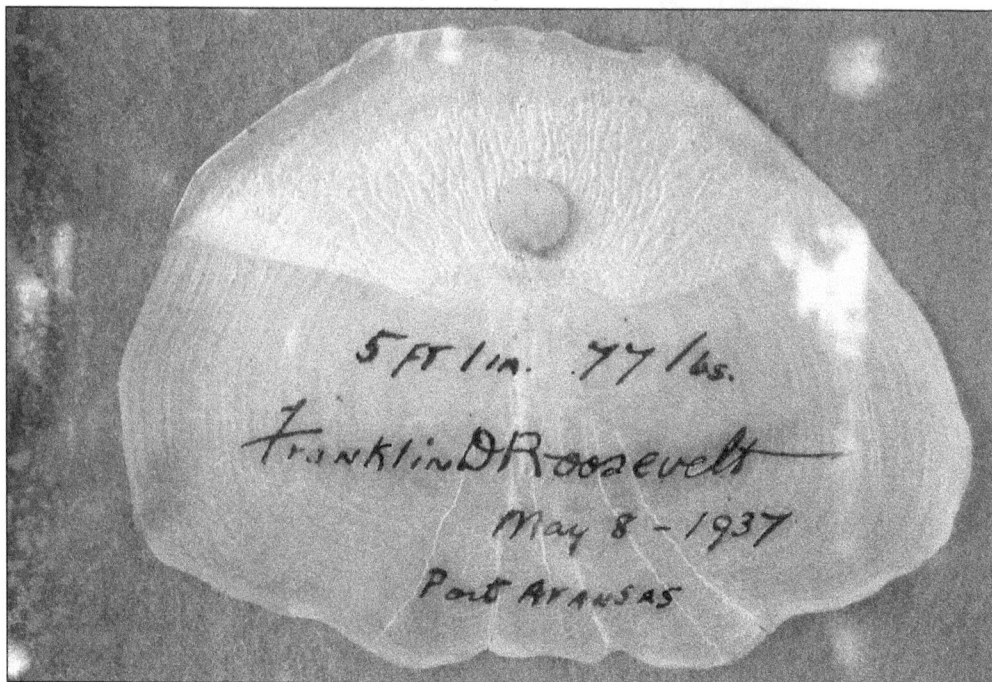

5 ft 1 in. 77 lbs.
Franklin D Roosevelt
May 8 - 1937
Port Aransas

While tarpon fishing was attracting fishermen to Port A, there were those sportsmen for whom the fishing intrigue lay farther offshore. The influence of these deep sea fishermen who pursued shark, sailfish, marlin, and dolphin (mahi-mahi) was strong enough that a second fishing tournament was warranted. The Deep Sea Roundup was held concurrently with the Texas Tarpon Rodeo in 1941. Like the rodeo, the Deep Sea Roundup began with a "hot start" from the dock (see above image). Note that these Farley boats have long port and starboard poles called outriggers, used for some types of deep sea fishing. The beautiful sailfish shown at left is eye candy to Deep Sea Roundup competitors. While the Texas Tarpon Rodeo ended in 1958, the roundup continues. It is now a nationally recognized saltwater tournament.

A chapter on Port Aransas fishing must include fishing stories. One such story is of Ted Mathews's party after a fisherman tied into a 6-foot tarpon. In his wild antics to throw the hook from his mouth, the fish leapt over the stern and landed squarely on top of the fisherman. The fellow was seriously injured, and as Mathews wrote, "suffered from his injuries for many years afterwards."

A bottlenose dolphin wildly jumped just 10 yards in front of a wade fisherman. The dolphin's behavior was to distract the fisherman from another dolphin that darted in and stole the fellow's stringer of speckled trout. The thief, with stringer in mouth, joined his accomplice and swam away with an easy meal. The fisherman believes this distract-and-pilfer tactic had to be the product of higher mental functioning.

Fourteen Foot
Hammer Head
Shark, Caught
by J. E. Cotter,
Port Aransas, Tex.

"Big fish" are notable events in any fishing environment and Port Aransas is no exception. The big fish story featuring the biggest fish are actually eyewitness testimonies—legally prepared affidavits—sent to the American Museum of Natural History in 1955. Three experienced fishermen swear that they observed a great white shark in excess of 24 feet—the length of their boat—1 mile off the Port Aransas beach. While those men did not have a camera, the Port Aransas fisherman who landed this 15-foot hammerhead shark was able to catch it on film. The image below is a sawfish—a misnomer because the creature is actually in the ray family—on the town docks. Whatever the classification, it is a huge sea creature.

Sawfish 16 ft 4 in long
16934 Port Aransas Tex

While being a big fish in its own right, this 6-foot, 6-inch tarpon proves the rule that there is always something bigger out there. In this case, a shark took a mouthful of a tarpon after it was hooked; the bite size puts the shark in excess of 13 feet.

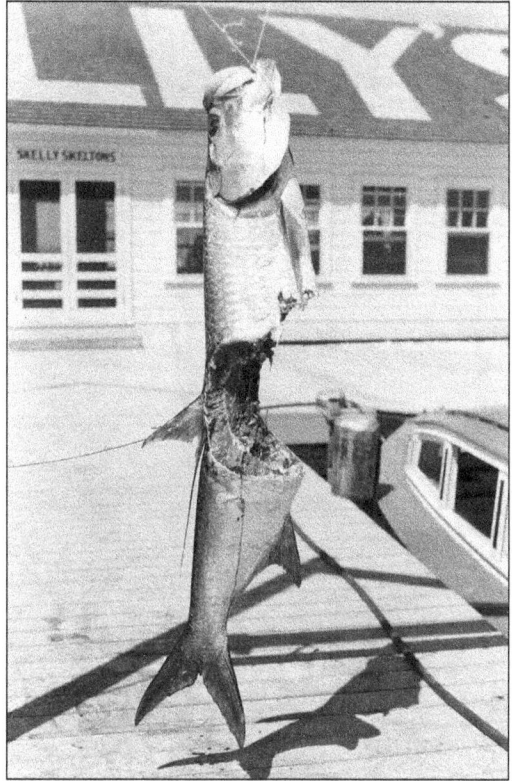

This 1937 photograph below shows George "Florida" Roberts, with hat in hand, looking at Barney Farley (far right). Both are icons of the fishing guide business. Roberts's fishing exploits were described in a book written by his wife, Elda May. In addition to being a skilled fisherman, Farley was an entrepreneur who truly advanced Port A's sport fishing industry. On Farley's kudos sheet is the cofounding of Texas's first saltwater fishing tournament, the Texas Tarpon Rodeo.

The fishing topic closes with this unique image. While the eye may first fall on the very respectable tarpon hanging from the upper deck of the Tarpon Inn, it does not take long to see that the fish is flanked by two lion clubs. The fisherman was circus star and owner Clyde Beatty. Beatty was the wild animal tamer who introduced the chair and bullwhip props. He came to Port Aransas to fish in 1953 and stayed at the Tarpon Inn. His companions were two young lions, no doubt on their way to stardom in the circus act. Not surprisingly, Beatty's visit was long remembered in Port Aransas.

Nine

ICONIC PORT ARANSAS

As the preceding chapters have shown, Mustang Island and Port Aransas have had evolving histories: settlers frontier, Civil War battleground, cattle ranch, fishing village, maritime town, military base, and tourist mecca. The authors thought that a meaningful way to end this book would be to provide images that are iconic of the Island and town's historical eras.

The 1857 lighthouse, for example, captures the essence of the settlement era on Mustang Island. The lighthouse marked the Aransas Pass for ships carrying supplies and new settlers, and this venerable structure was the scene of several Civil War actions. The 1904 Tarpon Inn is iconic of the area's early fishing days. Indeed, the very name of the hotel describes the creature responsible for first attracting mainlanders to Port Aransas. Some readers will look with nostalgia at the what locals called the old "turnout" causeway coming from the mainland to the ferry landing. Few images could better epitomize a child's anticipation and excitement of being just a few minutes away from a summer vacation of cane pole fishing and sand castle building in Port A.

Images do not have to be historical to possess iconic meaning. Large ships steaming through the Aransas Pass, a pelican on a piling, and the porch of Shorty's bar are, for example, current perceptions that give Port Aransas its wholly unique character and charm.

Be they past or present, on land or water, iconic images are compelling in their power to capture essences and stimulate memories. Enjoy.

Tarpon Inn, Port Aransas,
Formerly Tarpon, Tex.

Arguably the most significant Port Aransas feature is the Tarpon Inn. Frank Stephenson built this hostelry from a barrack in 1886. The original inn burned down in 1900 and was replaced in 1904 by the structure shown in the above photograph. That inn was wrecked by the 1919 storm and replaced in 1925 by the building shown below around 1942. The Tarpon Inn was at the heart of the early tarpon fishing days. It was there that fishermen rendezvoused with guides, took their meals, and slept. A persisting myth is that Pres. Franklin D. Roosevelt stayed at the inn. He did not, although a tarpon scale he autographed is displayed there.

Tarpon Inn
Port Aransas

The 1857 Aransas Pass Light Station is indicative of the settlement era. Ships bringing crucial supplies to settlers were guided to the Aransas Pass by this light. Deactivated in 1952, Charles Butt purchased the station in 1971 and restored it to the beautiful complex that is now called the Lydia Ann Lighthouse, shown here. The 55-foot-tall brick light tower is the original structure.

Station Port Aransas is pictured here in the 1940s. This is the longest-serving U.S. Coast Guard station on Mustang Island. It replaced the first station (see page 16) in 1925. This structure withstood six hurricanes and simply wore out in 1976. Personnel from this important facility safeguarded President Roosevelt's yacht in 1937, patrolled the beach for German infiltrators, and assisted in the evacuations of the 1961 and 1970 hurricanes.

In 1912, a railroad ran the 6 miles from the town of Aransas Pass to Harbor Island. By 1930, the need for that line ended, so the owners asphalted over the rail bed to create a causeway for cars. Harbor Island is where the Port Aransas ferryboats land. The causeway was a one-lane affair with pullouts to accommodate the two-way traffic. A $1 toll was collected at the booth shown below, looking from Aransas Pass toward Harbor Island. Replacing the piggyback railroad (page 56), the causeway was a boon to Port Aransas tourism. The ferry landing on Harbor Island can now be reached by a toll-free state highway that opened in late 1959.

Mainlanders coming to Port Aransas during the Great Depression made a good decision. The port had accepting townsfolk, a mild climate, potable water, and nutritious food was just a matter of learning to use the business end of a fishing pole. Folks who were down on their luck lived in an area called "Ragtown," so named for its tents. In the photograph above, these Ragtown children appear healthy and relatively happy. Below, the Gampert brothers, icons of Ragtown, pose in front of their tent with primitive fishing equipment.

Spiritual life is important in Port Aransas and is most recognizable by two structures. Saint Joseph Catholic Church, shown above under a rare blanket of snow, opened its doors around 1921. (It replaced the church lost in the 1919 hurricane.) A growing parish necessitated a larger structure. The old church is now privately owned, and while most of the pews were removed and a loft was added, the new owner preserved the steeple, original windows, and flooring. The Community Presbyterian Church, shown below, opened its doors in 1941, and the building still serves the congregation. This church is popular with folks wintering in Port Aransas. In fact, the Joint Effort Leisure Ministry community facility is on church grounds and serves as a venue for winter visitor activities.

Aline Carter, philanthropist and Texas poet laureate, gifted Port Aransas with this unique structure, the Chapel in the Dunes, in 1937. At prescribed times, Carter's chauffeur drove children to the chapel for Bible stories followed by ice cream and cake. The miniscule structure's 12 foot width made it a cozy place to be.

Barney Farley built the Rock Cottages motor court just prior to World War II, using rocks from the same San Antonio quarry that supplied rocks for the Aransas Pass jetties. These unique structures, icons of the early tourist era, have survived four major hurricanes and remain a popular spot to stay.

FORT WORTH STAR-TELEGRAM

EVENING HOME EDITION

Largest Circulation in Texas OVER 175,000 DAILY

Associated Press (Four Leased Wires)   A Fort Worth Owned Newspaper   International News Service

SIXTY-FIRST YEAR. No. 362.   FORT WORTH, TEXAS *** Where the West Begins *** WEDNESDAY, JANUARY 28, 1942.   TWENTY-TWO PAGES.   PRICE 3 CENTS

SUB SEEN OFF PORT ARANSAS

Another May Be Near By; Planes and Ships From Corpus Christi Are on Hunt

By Associated Press

CORPUS CHRISTI, Jan. 28.—Capt. Alva Bernhard, commander of the naval air station here, said Wednesday that a submarine, "doubtlessly German," had been sighted about 15 miles from Port Aransas Wednesday morning and there was a probability that another was nearby.

Planes and ships from the station are now seeking the craft, he said.

"The submarine is doubtless German and it probably sneaked in during the night with the intention of attacking oil tankers," Bernhard said.

The submarine was sighted by a naval air station plane on patrol, Bernhard said.

"It is possible that the second submarine is also in the vicinity since it is known that they have been operating in pairs elsewhere, and shortly after the submarine was sighted a smoke bomb appeared out of the water four miles south of it."

(Smoke bombs released by submarines, rise in the air similar to a rocket before settling back on the water. They frequently are used by submarines as a distress signal.)

The captain was unable to account for the smoke bomb other than through the possibility of its indicating a second craft.

Bernhard said the submarine was spotted by a patrol plane at 8:30 o'clock Wednesday morning.

While on patrol duty, the officers in the planes give navigation instruction to students. Bernhard said the plane reported the submarine and that he directed it to "maintain contact" with the undersea vessel. The navy plane was unarmed, he said.

"It evidently is..."

submarine was sighted.

On January 28, 1942, less than two months after the attack on Pearl Harbor, a U.S. Navy plane spotted a German U-boat close to the Aransas Pass jetties. This headline signaled that World War II had settled squarely into little Port Aransas. Among the alarms that went off was the concern that U-boats would land spies and saboteurs. To prevent that, the U.S. Coast Guard deployed personnel to monitor the Mustang Island coastline. The men of the beach patrol and their sentry dogs patrolled 24 hours a day, seven days a week. The island's beach, except for a small area close to the jetty, was off limits to unauthorized persons.

The strategic target for German submarines was an oil storage depot and oil tanker docks at nearby Harbor Island. A surfaced U-boat could come down the Aransas Pass at night and shell the storage tanks and torpedo the moored tankers; comparable attacks were made elsewhere during the war. To prevent such devastation, the army illuminated the pass by searchlights and placed two 155-milimeter (6-inch) cannons atop dunes just south of the jetty. The above photograph shows what had been one of the gun sites, a lasting indication of wartime Port Aransas. The coast artillery weapon was located on a raised platform, as illustrated in the photograph below of a 155-milimeter cannon precisely like the ones installed at Port Aransas. The coast artillery was an effective deterrent; the oil depot and tanker docks were never attacked.

After World War II, construction began on the Marine Science Institute, a facility for graduate education in the marine sciences. The above image shows the early stages of construction around 1947. The pier protrudes into the Aransas Pass, the structure at the end is the pier lab. The building with the front stairway was built in 1890 during construction of the jetties and serves today as a dormitory. Signage at the entrance to this educational facility makes clear its parent affiliation. It reads, "Marine Science Institute, The University of Texas at Austin." Below, the institute's teaching and research vessel, the *Longhorn*, is inspected by the university's mascot, Bevo. Both longhorns are now retired.

An iconic treatment of Port A would be incomplete without the town's oldest beer joint. Gladys "Shorty" Fowler opened Shorty's in 1946 in the Flats, the commercial area near the waterfront. This venerable watering hole is the venue for fun events, including an annual pig roast. On occasion, Shorty's was where singer and songwriter Patsy Jones performed. Shown below in her signature hat, this creative individual came to town in 1980. Jones soon found her niche as the resident performer by singing voice and playing acoustic guitar. Among her accomplishments was a song she wrote to celebrate life on Mustang Island. "That's My Island" was so popular that it was adopted as the official town song. Jones passed away in 2003, but her legacy as a representative of the Port Aransas entertainment scene will stand for a long time.

"When in Port Aransas get your picture standing in the mouth of the giant shark," is what a travel adviser writes. This giant shark is in front of the Destinations store on Alister Street. When this brute appeared in the 1990s, citizens were concerned that it was the harbinger of Port A becoming an overly commercialized tourist place—thankfully that has not yet occurred. As the image below so joyfully illustrates, there are some who could care less about such weighty town matters. The big shark means just one thing to them: big fun!

Not surprisingly, Port Aransas icons are also found in the marine environment. No water feature is more basic to Port Aransas than the Aransas Pass, which connects the Gulf of Mexico with the Corpus Christi ship channel. A variety of vessels transit the pass and channel, but none are more recognizable than the tanker ships. These vessels carry crude oil to the petroleum refineries at the Port of Corpus Christi, then transport refined products to various marketplaces. Dolphins leaping in front of vessels steaming through the pass is an engaging and symbolic image of Port Aransas. (Below, courtesy of Dan Parker and the *Port Aransas South Jetty* newspaper.)

To reach Port Aransas, the Corpus Christi ship channel must be crossed and, though it is narrow, the channel can be neither bridged nor tunneled. That means Port A will continue to be served by ferryboats, which have become an indelible part of the town character. In this iconic 1938 image, the entire fleet—the *Ruby, Estelle,* and *Nellie B*—steam their loads back and forth across the channel. There are now six 20-car ferries. This seafaring face below belongs to "Cap'n" James Taber, a ferryboat captain with a striking likeness to Popeye. Taber delighted passengers in the 1960s by performing his Popeye act on deck, contributing to what many people have described as the world's most enjoyable three-minute boat ride.

Extraordinarily large objects are iconic in Port Aransas. Like a colossal tinker toy, this quarter-mile long platform was fabricated by untold miles of steel tubing handled by 14 crane operators and teams of fitters and welders. The fabrication site, which has ceased operations, was on Harbor Island next to the current ferry landing. This particular platform was an offshore rig for drilling and recovering petroleum products from the Gulf of Mexico. The spectacle of a behemoth like this is even more enhanced when it is towed down the ship channel and out through the pass. Such an event is announced in town so that people can come and watch.

Bay fishing, which is such a large part of the Port Aransas fishing scene, offers two timeless symbols: natural gas platforms and little shrimp boats. The supporting legs of a platform are stabilized by a thick layer of oyster shells. This shell pad becomes home for little fish that attract game fish like speckled trout and black drum, making bay platforms potentially good fishing sites though the trick is finding the really productive ones. It is the little bay shrimp boat that supplies the town bait stands, but on occasion the shrimper itself becomes a stand. Fishermen needing to refill their bait wells while on the water pull up alongside a shrimper and usually get bait. The deal is often the classic coastal barter of beer for bait.

Pelican Line - Up, Port Aransas, Texas

Bird watching is an added benefit to fishing the bays. Thankfully the brown pelican has returned to the coast and it is no longer on the endangered species list. Uncontrolled pesticide usage once interfered with the pelicans' reproductive cycles. It is enjoyable to watch pelicans feeding. Their crashing dives into the water are entertaining, and fishermen use diving pelicans to point them to fish-rich waters. The roseate spoonbill, pictured below, is a wader that uses its spatulate bill to scoop up small fish and plant life along bay shorelines. A century ago, Port Aransans harvested these birds' pink feathers for women's hand fans. The roseate spoonbill now enjoys the elevated and safe status of being the official town bird.

This road sign once directed gamblers to the *Texas Treasure* dock. A converted European auto ferry, the *Texas Treasure* arrived in 2000 and moored next to the ferryboat landing on Harbor Island. The vessel was an example of getting around Texas's illegal casino gambling laws. Twice a day, the *Texas Treasure* steamed 9.2 miles offshore—just outside state jurisdiction—where it loitered for five hours as patrons dropped money into slot machines and tried their luck at casino games. The gambling ship was staffed by young people from the Caribbean who made a unique contribution to Port A life during their shore leaves. Mechanical difficulties and legal complications caused the *Texas Treasure* to fold her hand in 2008. With a new name on her stern, she is now plying the Mediterranean Sea.

Port Aransas possesses an iconic essence. When people live greatly isolated from the mainland, as was the case on Mustang Island from 1855 to 1926, they become self-reliant and bond closely as a group. Those two characteristics are evident in these images. After Hurricane Carla in 1961, residents did not wait for outside help. They began clearing away the debris to prepare for the rebuilding stage, which they also accomplished. This image at the community center captures the bonding of the townsfolk. Work together, play together, pray together. Such is the Port Aransas way.

Visit us at
arcadiapublishing.com

www.ingramcontent.com/pod-product-compliance
Lightning Source LLC
Chambersburg PA
CBHW050657150426
42813CB00055B/2211